The Acquisitive Streak

THE ACQUISITIVE STREAK

An Analysis of the Takeover and Merger
Boom

Christine Moir

Hutchinson Business

London   Melbourne   Auckland   Johannesburg

Hutchinson Business
An imprint of Century Hutchinson Ltd
62–65 Chandos Place, London WC2N 4NW

Century Hutchinson Publishing Group (Australia) Pty Ltd
16–22 Church Street, Hawthorn, Melbourne, Victoria 3122

Century Hutchinson Group (NZ) Ltd
32–34 View Road, PO Box 40–086, Glenfield, Auckland 10

Century Hutchinson Group (SA) Pty Ltd
PO Box 337, Bergvlei 2012, South Africa

First published 1986

Phototypeset in Linotron Sabon
by Input Typesetting, London
Printed and bound in Great Britain by
The Guernsey Press Co. Ltd,
Guernsey, Channel Islands

British Library Cataloguing in Publication Data
Moir, Christine
    The acquisitive streak: an analysis of
    the takeover and merger boom.
    1. Consolidation and merger of corporations
    ——Great Britain
    I. Title
    338.8′3′0941   HD2746.5

ISBN 0–09–167721–1 Pbk

Contents

1 **Merger Mania**   1

Newspapers — Widening Appetite —
Fuelling the Appetite — Obsession —
Conclusion

2 **The Beginning**   19

Thomas Tilling — Eagle Star —
Arbitrageurs — Conclusion

3 **£1 Billion and Beyond**   35

Dee Corporation — GEC — Conclusion

4 **The Raiders**   46

Sir Ralph Halpern — Lord Hanson — Sir
Owen Green — James Gulliver

5 **The Prey**   62

Distillers — Tootal — Fleet — Woolworth
— Allied Lyons — Conclusion

6 **The Backers**   80

Merchant Bankers — Lawyers — Brokers
— Accountants — Publicists

7 **The Shareholders**   101

Institutions — Individuals — Financial
Climate — Targeting — Rank
Organisation

8 **Tactics**   112

Management Buyouts — Poison Pills —
Greenmail — Libel — Professionals —
Junk Bonds — Morgan Crucible —
Trusthouse Forte — Conclusion

9 **The City**   131

Britannia Arrow — Jacob Rothschild —
Lloyds — Mercantile — Conclusion

10 **Prospects and Warnings**   145

Sir Gordon Borrie — Regulation —
Hanson Trust — Storehouse — Argyll —
Foster — Cover Up — Precedents —
Conclusion

Index   164

1

Merger Mania

In January 1975 the stockmarket picked itself up from the floor and launched a bull market which is still running more than 11 years later. A combination of the 1974 oil crisis, enormous imprudent bank lending on property development which led to the notorious secondary banking crisis of the same year, and the near-failure of Burmah Oil, which had to be rescued by the Bank of England, sent the Financial Times Index crashing to 146 over the 1974–5 New Year period. It looked as if Britain was about to relive 1929 after its own, domestic stock-market crash.

By great good fortune a financial Armaggedon was averted. Within a fortnight the Index had begun to respond to the concerted efforts of a handful of leading institutions to restore it to health. At the request of the Bank of England, which had already made its move to rescue the secondary banks, the institutions agreed to show confidence in the clean-up operation by buying heavily in the market.

The success of their mission could truly be measured only a decade later in April 1985 when the same index was standing at just below 1000 and poised to go dramatically higher. In between there were some difficult periods if no real setbacks. One of these occurred in the early 1980s as the result of a severe recession affecting the entire industrialized world from the end of 1979. During a period of some three years markets languished; the majority of shares marked time. But the breathing space heralded the approach of something quite new even in this long bull market—invasion by predators.

Newspapers

In Britain the notion of owning a newspaper has always held a fatal fascination for certain kinds of business tycoons. Neither the general lack of profitability or prospects, nor the diminishing influence of newspapers in a television dominated society seems seriously to diminish the attraction. Newspaper proprietorship is something captains of industry simply lust after.

The greatest newspaper takeover of modern times—of *The Times* by the Australian Rupert 'The Dirty Digger' Murdoch—took place in the late 1970s. In the mid-1980s Murdoch was playing a different sort of game in the UK; defeating the power of the mighty but obsolete print unions. He had moved *The Times* and the *Sunday Times*, into a new building on the banks of the Thames, at Wapping in East London. It was a gesture of defiance against the print unions which ruled the Fleet Street area and which he had sacked en masse just ahead of the move to Wapping. There were immense difficulties in the move, not least the problems of bedding down *The Times*' journalistic staff with those who manned Murdoch's mass market tabloid newspaper, the *Sun*. Murdoch's interests spanned the US and Australia as well as Britain, and abroad he had not given up making acquisitions. In the US his concentration appeared to become fixed on television stations and companies. In pursuit of his aim to be a mogul of the small screen he even changed his nationality from Australian to American, since US laws permit only nationals to own the most important medium of communication.

Being abroad however, Murdoch's acquisitive habits in

the 1980s lie outside the scope of this book. This does not leave us bereft of newspaper proprietors and would be proprietors to follow during this period. Far from it; the urge to collect a newspaper had not deserted British industrialists, even those who had done it before without any palpable increase in their wealth or status to show for it. Among the most interesting of the newspaper takeovers of the mid-1980s must be included Robert Maxwell's acquisition of the Mirror Group; the absorption of the old Beaverbrook empire of Express Newspapers within the collection of United Newspapers, publishers of the *Yorkshire Post* and *Punch* magazine; and Tiny Rowland's appetite for yet more punishment by taking 35 per cent and effective control of the languishing infant, *Today* newspaper. Each reinforced the view that buying a newspaper is not a rational business decision but a symptom of acquisitiveness; that newspapers exert a magnetic force upon those suffering from such acquisition fever.

Robert Maxwell

The case of Robert Maxwell was a curious one. For years this Czech-born entrepreneur had combined technical and scientific magazine publishing through his privately owned Pergamon Press with newspaper printing. At the turn of the decade he had used his private wealth to rescue the British Printing and Publishing Corporation (BPCC) which was probably the major contract printer to the newspaper industry.

Maxwell, although a colourful and controversial figure, had never shaken off a 1960s tag attached to him in a Board of Trade inquiry into his acquisition of Pergamon, that he was 'unfit to run a public company'. But, although excluded from the Establishment he was at least an established figure in the newspaper supply industry. As such he appeared resistant to the fascination of newspapers themselves. There were always rumours that Maxwell wanted to own a paper, but each time the rumour gained credence Maxwell would roundly declare that his interest lay in printing not publishing national titles.

At the beginning of the 1980s that excuse seemed to wear thin and it soon became clear that Maxwell had indeed joined the ranks of those who thirst to be press barons. One early sign came when he competed to buy the *Observer*, the independent, liberal-inclined Sunday which had briefly fallen into the hands of Atlantic Richfield, a US energy group which was expanding into North Sea oil exploration.

Atlantic Richfield had soon come to the realization that wanting a stake in the Brent oil market did not mean it needed to embrace all things British, particularly a loss-making newspaper whose international coverage leaned towards the African not American continent. But, as ever, others did want the *Observer*. A battle ensued which Maxwell fought with great vigour but without success. The *Observer* was sold to 'Tiny' Rowland, the chief executive of the Lonrho Group who was also still chasing acceptance by the Establishment after forty years of running the Lonrho Anglo-African trading and manufacturing group.

Maxwell retreated to continue printing newspaper supplements at BPCC. A minor purchase of the specialist financial newspaper, *Financial Weekly*, was the only sign that his urge to be a press baron had not died. There were also constant plans to launch a newspaper but these did not bear fruit.

Then, in 1984 the great title of the *Express* came on the market. Express newspapers, which still bore the stamp of their founder, the legendary Lord Beaverbrook, had become part of Trafalgar House, a construction and property group, during the 1970s. The mix did not prove successful and the Express Group was spun off from Trafalgar, eventually to be renamed Fleet Holdings. Already by 1984 Fleet looked as if it would not last long as an independent quoted company. Predators were sizing it up, amongst them Robert Maxwell.

4

This time Maxwell did not disguise his eagerness. The *Express* was a worthy prize. However, in a number of confusing moves not yet adequately explained, Maxwell also threw his hat into the ring for that old Labour war horse, the *Mirror*. Maxwell must have known that Government competition policy would never allow him to own both. Yet, as he was building a stake in the *Express* to around 15 per cent he was also in competition against the management to buy the *Mirror* from Reed International, its paper and packaging parent.

Maxwell narrowly won this tussle — by outbiding the management — and was forced to leave the *Express* to United Newspapers, which yearned to join the Fleet Street tycoons whom it saw as somehow superior to its own provincial status (United Newspapers publishes the *Yorkshire Post*). Maxwell, who enjoys being described as a socialist despite his millions, soon found that having a common political persuasion did not make the *Mirror* a tractable possession. By late 1985 his battles with the *Mirror's* print unions had made him declare that he had failed to turn the paper round and would close it. Like so many other statements from the Maxwell camp, however, this too appeared more of an emotional outburst than a serious declaration of intent. The *Mirror* struggled along; so too did rumours that Maxwell planned to launch a new title.

By now the idea of launching new newspapers on the back of labour-saving technology had taken hold across a broad front. There were plans for a new Labour Party paper to begin in the autumn despite a long tradition which proved that left wing politics rarely made for flourishing papers. A right of centre paper, to be called the *Independent*, had been spawned by the former city editor of the *Daily Telegraph*, and was also straining towards an October start. Ahead of the field was *Today*, the downmarket colour newspaper which had got off to a shaky start in March 1986. Other ideas for new titles were also brewing.

For all this activity the old game of buying newspapers still went on. When the *Telegraph* was in difficulty a young Canadian entrepreneur, Conrad Black, took a minority stake to help out. In fact it soon became clear that Black's notion of helping out was to help himself to the *Telegraph*. He soon had 51 per cent, a new chief executive in the shape of the former editor of the *Economist*, and two new editors at the *Daily Telegraph* and *Sunday Telegraph*.

Tiny Rowland

Then it was the turn of Tiny Rowland once more. Lonrho had beaten Maxwell for the *Observer* in 1981 but Rowland could not gloat over victory for long. The *Observer* not only persistently lost money, it also espoused policies which hurt Lonrho's important African connections. Yet the structure of the paper, which was hedged about with independent directors and the personal strength of its editor, denied Tiny the pleasure of having his own paper reflect his own interests.

Galling as this must have been it did not appear to diminish Rowland's appetite for the newspaper industry. When Eddie Shah needed to re-finance *Today* in early June, Rowland was among those queuing, together with Maxwell again, to provide the funds. This time, for a price somewhere between £15 and £20 million, he obtained only 35 per cent of *Today*. Technically he was a minority shareholder, which neatly avoided any problems with the Office of Fair Trading which automatically studies all newspaper takeovers. But few believed that Rowland would be content with passive investment for long, or indeed for anything other than outright control. Rowland too visibly had been bitten by the newspaper bug.

Widening Appetite

Had the takeover urge remained concentrated in the newspaper sector the mid-1980s would not have been particularly remarkable. True, there appeared to be more tycoons than usual wanting to become press barons. But Fleet Street is an hermetic industry—as witness its special labour relations problems. What happens in Fleet Street rarely infects the rest of industry.

What made it clear that something unusual was going on was that the great newspaper struggles were relegated to the inside pages even of the newspapers themselves. The major takeover stories were happening elsewhere, in the heartlands of commerce and industry, and even in the City itself. An acquisitive streak had surfaced in British industry which had not been seen on such a scale since 1968.

Every so often stockmarkets go crazy. Share prices rear up or plunge out of all proportion to the fortunes of the underlying companies they represent. Usually such bouts of madness die out as swiftly as they are born. Within weeks the indices assume more normal trends; flatter angles are restored to the graphs; before long only a brief bulge in the records marks the passing of the fever.

There are times however when the underlying industrial and commercial trends are themselves just sufficiently unusual to give some credibility to the antics of the stock-market carousel. Then, instead of a few brief weeks of investor fever, both industry and investment become locked in a dizzy embrace which seems to have no end.

One such period occurred in Britain in 1984. It was still running in the middle of 1986. In fact bid fever held most of the world's securities markets in its grip during that time. In part the British version mirrored this international tendency. One of the most frequently repeated excuses for takeovers was the perceived need to become big enough to compete against much larger American or Japanese—or even European—concerns in international markets. But the bid fever which spread to Britain was no mere pale reflection of what was taking place elsewhere. Britain's entrepreneurs had discovered or rediscovered an acquisitive streak and were burning to deploy it.

Takeovers are one of the ways in which the capital markets ensure that commercial assets continue to be efficiently managed. They form an integral part of a healthy market. Starting in 1983, though more particularly in 1984, 1985 and into 1986, the number and scale of bids had grown vastly beyond the levels seen for the past 15 years.

In 1983 bids worth £2.3 billion were successfully concluded. In 1984 that figure had risen to £5.5 billion. Because takeovers are such a normal corporate function some commentators continued to blind themselves to what was happening. Even the influential Lex column of the *Financial Times* was happy to note the growth in takeovers and wish more companies could be shaken out of torpor. By 1985, when the bid total had grown to £7.1 billion and several billions more were in train, even the most myopic could see that the trend was quite extraordinary.

It was not just the number of takeovers or their size which revealed how different the corporate world had become. It was also the intensity with which the attacks were mounted and resisted and the way in which a handful of professional predators made the headlines. It was the fact also that many companies continued to grasp for growth by acquisition while surrounded with evidence from their own, or from competitors', recent experience that acquisitions frequently cause more headaches than they cure. In short there was incontrovertible evidence that a fever had gripped the business community which made captains of industry lust to collect any corporate entity within sight whether logic supported the venture or not.

Retailing

The acquisitive urge spread to every industrial sector. It was somehow appropriate that some of the most highly publicized and bitter battles should take place in the store groups. In retailing, with the possible exception of Marks & Spencer over whom Divine Providence keeps watch, no one stays king of the heap for long. The High Street is in constant flux as each of its inhabitants seeks the secret of perpetual motion. In the consumer world to stand still is to die. Fashions must be constantly renewed; that is the nature of fashion. The group which does not feed the maw of fashion with a regular flow of new ideas is soon relegated to the dust heap.

In this environment the hyper-activity of someone like Ralph Halpern, head of the Burton Group, might have been relatively inconspicuous. In some ways Halpern is merely obeying the law of the High Street: grow or die. As discussed further in Chapter 4 the speed with which he set about taking over his targets, and the size of each mouthful, drew all eyes. Were all these moves part of a coolly planned commercial policy or evidence of a simpler lust for personal power?

Even as Halpern, and others like him in the retailing sector, were collecting other retailers as fast as they could, the evidence was all about that retailing takeovers could be a very risky business. BAT Industries which has more recently embarked upon a series of acquisitions in the financial services areas, had earlier picked on retailing as a major diversification from tobacco. By 1986 its struggling International Stores supermarket chain had already passed to the Dee Corporation, newest star in food retailing. BAT was also breaking up and selling BATUS, its US retailing arm which had been an especially disappointing acquisition.

In the early stages of the takeover boom a number of non-retailers had also been seduced into making takeovers in the retail sector. Most famous was probably Lord Hanson of Hanson Trust, a conglomerate based mainly on industrial investments. While Hanson's true interests remained with the less spectacular parts of British industry he had the most highly developed acquisitive streak of any British industrialist. It was probably this which induced him to enter the bid battle for UDS in 1982.

Hanson's takeover tactics are highly refined and do not

end when the bid itself is completed. After he won control of UDS there came a series of break-ups and sales of parts of the group which left only the Allders department store chain. But that was still not the end of the matter. By 1986 the massaging effects of the original takeover had evaporated and Allders' profits had begun to flag again. Hanson was forced into another series of break-ups and sales.

Brewing

If takeovers are natural in retailing the same cannot be said of such bastions of permanence and stability as the brewing of beer and distilling of spirits. Yet during the mid-1980s appetites were no less voracious among the brewers and distillers than in the haberdashers' halls. Indeed the drinks sector furnished some of the most costly banquets of the entire period. The great billion pound battles for Distillers and Allied Breweries provide material for nearly every chapter of this book. For the bidders—Guinness and the Australian Elders IXL—no doubt their prey was worth every penny of the cost. For outsiders it was difficult to shake off a nagging doubt. Distillers' board had indeed become moribund and deserved to go. How much improvement Guinness could wring out of the underlying business was an open question. World consumption of whisky is in decline and Distillers makes more Scotch than anyone else. Allied Breweries is a different matter. It is still a fast-moving and ambitious company and already the second largest brewer in the UK. It will need to run very fast to make a discernible impact on current profit growth.

Sugar Industry

Companies which had tilted unsuccessfully at each other as recently as the early 1980s were prepared to repeat the process all over again even in the face of almost certain reference to the Monopolies Commission.

10

Tate & Lyle, the cane sugar group, seemed to have that approach to British Sugar, which has an effective monopoly of the UK beet sugar business. In 1981 the battle between Tate and British Sugar was one of the most complex ever seen in Britain. There were cross-shareholdings between various companies designed to make one or other unpalatable at any time; there were arguments of impenetrable learnedness which sought to prove that no monopoly existed in any area. Eventually the Monopolies Commission professed itself unimpressed with any of the arguments and British Sugar found itself a subsidiary of S & W Berisford, the commodity group.

In 1986 Tate was burning to have another attempt at the prize. Hillsdown Holdings, a food company recently spun off from the Imperial Group and spreading its wings, bid for Berisford in the spring of 1986. Tate, which admitted that it only wanted British Sugar, not the rest of Berisford's tricky commodity operations, could not hold out and also put in a bid. Once again a third party turned up, this time in the shape of Ferruzzi, the large Italian agricultural concern which waited in the wings.

Ephraim Margulies, Berisford's powerful chairman was determined to keep Berisford whole and independent. In pursuit of this end he pleaded for the two bids to be investigated by the Monopolies Commission and he caused a bitter internal row by resisting hopes cherished by Gordon Percival, managing director of the British Sugar subsidiary, for a management buyout.

'Marg', as he is familiarly called in the City, won his reference to the Monopolies Commission. At that stage things began to get really interesting. Hillsdown displayed normal commonsense, sold its 28 million shares in Berisford to Ferruzzi for a fat profit and went off looking for something easier to capture. Tate could not shake off its obsession with British Sugar and determined to see out the bid reference. The role Ferruzzi was playing remained inscrutable. Some thought it was only acting as an arbitrageur, trying to force Tate to bid higher so it could get

11

out at a profit. The Monopolies reference, meanwhile, put the entire game on 'hold' until the end of the year. So only Hillsdown was free to enjoy its profits.

One of the more bizarre elements in this was that newcomers had difficulty understanding British Sugar's attractiveness in the mid-1980s. The world had changed since 1981. Commodity prices had slumped dramatically; sugar was among the hardest hit. Old hopes that controlling 90 per cent of the UK sugar industry would provide a basis for burgeoning international profits had crumbled with world sugar prices of less than 5 cents a pound. As Tate continued to pursue British Sugar in the face of these realities, it became crystal clear that its bid was not a piece of cool business strategy but a passion. Tate had hungered for British Sugar for years; no change in world market conditions could affect that sort of hunger.

Engineering

Fixation and obsession were one side of the acquisitive urge; the continuous triumph of hope over experience was another. Heavy engineering companies tend to perform, even in their best years, at a fairly predictable rate; they might be said to have a certain cruising speed. Thus when the bull market boiled over in the 1986 New Year but refused to turn into a significant bear trend, the one sector fundamentalists believed would go quiet was engineering.

They were wrong. In May Glynwed, best known as a manufacturer of baths and other household engineered products, was bidding for Brickhouse Dudley which makes manhole covers and drainage pipes. Valve-maker, Pegler Hattersley, was undergoing an increased offer out of the more broadly based industrial holding group, F. H. Tomkins. One of housebuilder C. G. Beazer's subsidiary suppliers was pitching for Benford Concrete whose speciality is making concrete mixers and cement silos. There were others.

Given the fact that most of these targets were in sectors

where sudden growth could not be expected, the prices being paid were hard to justify. At the heaviest end of British industry average share prices represented some 14 years of earnings at current levels.

Fuelling the Appetite

Without any doubt the high share prices of the raging bull market were interwoven with the bid fever of the time. What is more difficult is to try and unravel the relationship. Were share prices high because of the constant presence of predators, or were the predators sucked into the market by the bull trend in shares? Fundamentalists might argue that predators should stay away from a bull market; the time to buy is when shares are cheap. The fundamentalists would be right—if all bids were made for cash. One of the hallmarks however of the later stages of this bout of bid fever was the use of paper rather than cash. Companies bid for others with their own shares, and these, of course, had soared with the rest of the market.

It was certainly true that the great leg of the bull market which swept the Financial Times 30-Share Index up to an all-time peak of 1425.9 on 3 April 1986, had started before the first signs of merger mania appeared in mid-1983. It was also true that the market set-back which went on into the early summer, did not deter the predators who were already embarked on takeovers at the time. A degree of untidiness at the edges was only to be expected, however, and does not disprove the theory that the bull market depended on bid fever just as much as the fever was fuelled by the buoyancy of share prices.

The rise in share prices benefited the predators as much as their prey. It made it easier for the attackers to use their own shares in takeover bids. This became a major factor during the takeover boom; with each passing year, as shares continued to soar, so less and less cash was used in bid battles. The way in which the boom in takeovers sustained and supported the bull market is even more interesting if harder to prove beyond doubt.

In the spring of 1986, when the FT Index broke back down from its peak of over 1400 a major reaction was expected. National Westminster Bank's huge £700+ million rights issue was the immediate cause although there were other reasons. Economic prospects both at home and abroad were more confused than they had been; while the sunshine had not been driven away the climate for industry had certainly turned more showery. Changeable weather does not sustain the sort of bull market which occurred between January and April when the index rose by nearly 40 per cent from an already high base. Other rights issues and a further Government campaign of privatizations promised to take up institutional funds well into the autumn. Yet the index never penetrated through 1300 right up to mid-summer.

Something other than industrial outlook or inherent momentum seemed to be sustaining the market at this time. The continuing activity on the takeover front, though not as frenetic as it had been in the New Year and early spring, was the most obvious cause. Just as high share prices seemed to conceal from the protagonists in bids just how risky a venture they were engaged upon, so the willingness of entrepreneurs to pay enormous prices for their targets persuaded the market that the downside for shares should be limited. The two trends fed upon each other.

This much had been apparent since mid-1984. Each bid milestone brought another wave of share price rises which, in turn, persuaded a new round of predators that high bid prices could be justified. The spiral confirmed shareholders in their belief that their own company's market value could only increase, an emotional state which lent stoutness to defence as much as spirit to attack.

Few companies were, in fact, able to resist a determined attack; the number which walked away independent and unscathed from an unwanted bid diminished each year.

14

But defending shareholders were right in so far that take-overs did not come cheap; a stout defence almost invariably forced the bidder to up the price to a significant degree.

The willingness with which bidders were prepared to increase their original offers was one of the most telling features of this boom, and the one which most revealed it as a product of feverish emotion rather than compelling industrial logic. Prudent commercial planning rests in large measure on putting a firm price on any potential purchase. To be sure takeover tactics might dictate a sighting shot somewhat below this price. But during the takeover boom of the mid-1980s bidders seemed prepared to go on increasing their offers until they simply ran out of time under Takeover Code rules. Moreover, in almost no case was the increase accompanied by solid explanations. At best some vaguely outlined improvement in prospects was appealed to.

Obsession

A further clue to the nature of this era of takeovers came from the manner in which they were conducted. Regulatory authorities and dispassionate on-lookers complained that bids launched during this time were pursued with an intensity and commitment not seen since the late 1960s. This was a euphemistic way of saying that they were carried out with such emotional intensity that scant attention was paid to the rules. Those rules, encapsulated in the Takeover Code, had not been formulated by the late 1960s. In large measure they were the authorities' reaction to the ruthlessness of those late 1960s bid battles. Now, the City authorities feared, the rules which had stood the test of nearly 20 years, were being assailed by more vigorous buffeting than they had been designed to withstand.

As it transpired the City Code was more resilient than the authorities had feared. There were undoubted transgressions; some of its rules had to be rewritten to extend to new tactics which had been unknown to the original draftsmen; appeals against the Takeover Panel's decision were a frequent and unpleasant feature of most contested bids; there were hints that the forthcoming change in the structure of City regulation under the 1987 Financial Services Act could leave the voluntary Takeover Code high and dry. But for the meantime the Code held; the Panel's rulings were still expected to apply.

If the passionate intensity of the 1980s predators, with their sharp, new practices, did not manage to destroy the City Code, some might argue that it was not for want of trying. As discussed further in Chapter 6, the aristocratic manners of the merchant banks are worn for convenience only. In pursuit of their clients' interests (which in turn line their own pockets) they will bend the rules very far indeed. Chapter 8, which looks at the tactics used during takeovers reinforces how far the principals themselves were prepared to go in order to win.

But the single most important effect of this emotional involvement was the way it blinded bidders to the wisdom of their ventures. Cool judgement dictates that the bidder put a ceiling on the price he is prepared to pay. He must walk away if that ceiling is reached. Between 1984 and 1986 few bids were called off because the bidder refused to up the ante. Either most bidders set very high ceilings to their target prices or the notion of a definite ceiling had dissolved in the heat of battle.

It was difficult to avoid the suspicion that the latter represented the truth of it. Bidders could be virtually assured of success if they only paid enough. When emotions are at fever pitch 'enough' can always be made to look a modest enough sum. In the spring of 1986 Stanley Kalms of Dixons persuaded himself that Woolworth was worth a bid of £1.25 billion. Outsiders were aghast. Not twelve months before its market value had been not much more than half that sum. By early June Kalms had upped his offer to £1.9 billion. The first figure was enormous enough, reckoned against Dixons' own size. The question arises as to whether Kalms planned all along to go much higher or was he simply trapped by his desire to outface Woolworth's institutional shareholders?

The emotions which drive predators at all times and in all periods were fuelled by the special pressures of the mid-1980s. Lord Weinstock, chief executive of the General Electric Company, has a reputation for extreme coolness under fire. During the late 1970s and early 1980s he launched GEC on a number of bids only to pull out the moment he thought the price was beginning to overheat. That pattern, even more than GEC's own ability to generate cash, was responsible for the £1.5 billion which had piled up in GEC's reserves by the middle of the decade.

Suddenly everything seemed to change. Chapter 2 examines in more detail GEC's bid of just over £1 billion for Plessey, important for at least two reasons. First it was presented as a response to the demands of internationalism — grow big enough or keep out, and secondly because it also appeared to show Weinstock deserting his normal principles of prudence and caution. In bidding for Plessey, 'the Blessed Arnold' (as he is known in the City) seemed as passionately committed to winning as any of the obvious hotheads in town.

The siren call of internationalism was also being heard in the City, itself in the throes of revolutionary change. According to those who led the Stock Exchange, survival meant adopting internationally-accepted free-for-all trading methods. For practitioners the key factor was size. Both claims worked together so that by early 1986 only one of the top 20 stockbroking firms had not been taken over by a non-broker.

Even the clearing banks became obsessed with internationalism, and at least one with the idea that it must grow still larger in order to compete internationally. For the most part, however, the clearers contented themselves with small but strategic purchases which they hoped would give them an internationally acceptable range of financial services. Few of these purchases qualified for inclusion in this study but the strategy of Lloyds Bank certainly did. In pursuit of what it saw as international size Lloyds mounted a billion pound bid for Standard Chartered. The irony of this was that Standard was still smarting from its own failed attempt to take over Royal Bank of Scotland a handful of years before. Now it found itself repeating many of Royal's arguments about lack of fit and incompatible temperament.

Conclusion

Not every takeover during this time was characterized by obsession. Most were still planned and executed as part of a careful corporate strategy. By the time the Director General of the Office of Fair Trading came to write his report on 1985 he was forced to point up the hysteria and feverishness which had crept into so many bid battles. There was no denying it: logic had flown out of a number of boardroom windows to be replaced by emotion.

It could be argued that the acquisitive streak which was aroused in so many entrepreneurs as industry climbed out of recession in 1983, became unhealthy because it blinded too many to the uncertainty of acquisitions as a route to growth. The evidence was all around — in the corpses left over from the last bout of merger mania in the early 1970s or the flagging fortunes of former high fliers bought even more recently. A hyper-active acquisition strategy also absorbed the energies which should have been devoted to careful corporate husbandry. Takeover targets, of course, had no choice but to abandon their proper business in order to try to see off the raiders.

2

The Beginning

One of the earliest signs that takeovers had become increasingly important was BTR's exceptionally large £660 million bid for Thomas Tilling in the spring of 1983. This bid, made for an acknowledged leader in its field, was bitterly contested by Tilling's board whose advisers were none other than the merchant bankers, S. G. Warburg. Despite this and the fact that it had no obvious industrial logic to compel it, it succeeded, and in doing so ushered in the takeover era in which no company, however large or successful, could feel safe from a raider.

Thomas Tilling

If there was ever a case of the hunter turned hunted, this was it. Thomas Tilling may have begun life in the last century as a horse bus operator, but shortly after the Second World War it sold its London Red Bus business, the proceeds of which funded a quite different form of expansion. Tilling became, largely through a succession of risky but successful acquisitions, a highly diversified industrial holding company. By the mid-1960s Tilling was forcing dramatic growth out of a collection of businesses which ranged from Heinemann, the publishers, through Cornhill Insurance and Pretty Polly tights to heavy industrial engineering. Pre-tax profits grew from £4.3 million to £12.9 million and there was more growth to come. Further acquisitions which took place throughout the 1970s culminated in some major investments in the US energy field, and led profit growth to a peak of £81.1 million in 1979.

This diversification into the US was intended to remedy what had been perceived for some time as Tilling's over-dependence on the fitful British economy. Certainly in 1980 and 1981 the US subsidiaries counter-balanced some of the shortfall, as the UK businesses became affected by the recession. By 1982 it became clear that the high-risk end was in fact those very American investments which had been made to limit the risk. The damage caused by sudden losses in the US energy equipment company was visible in the accounts and profits had slumped to £43.7 million.

At this period Tilling was masterminded by Sir Patrick Meaney, an urbane and gentlemanly accountant by profession, who was a leading figure in the CBI and well known throughout industry. In addition to his job as managing director of Tilling, Sir Patrick was also deputy chairman of Midland Bank and on a number of other boards. When Tilling's profit growth faltered in 1980 Sir Patrick was the first to admit that: "We are now vulner-able". By the time the 1982 profit collapse was unveiled Tilling had become a natural takeover victim although it was trying desperately to make itself too large to be a victim, by concentrating upon growth by acquisition itself.

Owen Green (now Sir Owen), the chief executive of BTR, could not be more different from Sir Patrick. Where Sir Patrick has a wide range of commercial, artistic and leisure interests outside his main job, Green lists nothing but BTR in his *Who's Who* entry. Where Sir Patrick ran Tilling in a gentlemanly hands off fashion from an 18th century aristocrat's mansion in Mayfair, Green and his small central office team were practising direct inter-vention from their spartan base in Victoria.

From the outset it was clear that this would be a battle

of management styles. No amount of oratory could make it appear that Tilling's collection of companies fitted naturally with BTR's own heterogeneous but mostly manufacturing based businesses. Tilling's shareholders, largely institutions, had merely to decide whether they thought Green could wring more profits out of the collection than Sir Patrick. On that front Tilling's position as an industrial conglomerate told against Sir Patrick.

The success or failure of conglomerates is difficult to understand with market analysts often hesitant to interpret their results. Many of these conglomerates flourish while others perish, others prove successful for long periods then suddenly cease to perform. If this was what had happened at Tilling it might be possible that a complete change in management style could revive its fortunes. Eventually just enough of the institutions were prepared to accept this solution and BTR's bid of £660 million was finally successful. Sir Patrick Meaney received ample consolation and within weeks the institutions had installed him in the chairman's seat at Rank Organisation, from where they had just forcibly ejected the autocratic but ageing Sir John Davis. Sir Patrick's task was to find an energetic and talented successor as chief executive but ultimately the institutions were prepared to see Sir Patrick retain the top seat reinforced by a new financial genius, Michael Gifford, one rung down.

Interest in BTR's bid for Tilling was not centred exclusively on the central characters of Green and Sir Patrick. This bid was also important for marking the emergence of Morgan Grenfell as the foremost merchant bank in contested bid battles, and for the high profile forced on Tilling's institutional shareholders. By winning Tilling for its clients, BTR, Morgan Grenfell scored an important victory over its major rival, S. G. Warburg, and laid the foundation for the next three years when it was ranked first among its peers as an adviser in takeovers. For the institutional shareholders the battle was a much more uncomfortable period. Britain's great pension funds and

21

insurance companies like to plead that they are no more participants in the companies they invest in than the smallest private investor, but both BTR and Tilling appealed directly to the institutions and between them BTR had narrowly the better of the argument.

Green's main asset was the sparkling profits performance he unveiled at precisely the right moment. Just as his rival was having to admit to a catastrophic 1982 profits slump, Green unveiled figures which, for the first time, topped Tilling's previous peak. Moreover he had squeezed profits of around £107 million out of sales only about one-third of Tilling's £2.2 billion. Yet, as the bid progressed, Sir Patrick forecast a complete recovery in Tilling's growth — to a new peak of £95 million in 1983.

Some of the institutions made a public virtue out of supporting good management on the defensive, the Prudential among them. The BTR bid was a test of their resolve, a test which by some standards, they failed. Green achieved his success by the narrowest of margins (barely over 50 per cent), and then only after his advisers had bought 9 per cent of Tilling in the market. It was however still the institutions which gave Tilling to BTR for had they refused Green's bid would have failed. The institutions spouted explanations, excuses and justifications for months afterwards, but it was hard to avoid the thought that they too were suffering from bid fever by this time and could no longer keep to a long-term investment philosophy now that such good short-term profits were being offered to them.

Eagle Star

BTR's bid for Thomas Tilling was not destined to remain in the record books for long. By the autumn of 1983 an international battle had developed for Eagle Star, Britain's sixth largest insurance group. By the time that battle had reached the last round the numbers being talked of quite dwarfed the £660 million BTR takeover bid for Tilling.

It all started in October 1983 when the German insurance giant, Allianz, sprang a surprise bid on Eagle Star, a large but otherwise unremarkable British composite insurer. At £692 million, or 500p a share, Allianz's offer was not ungenerous for an insurance group with premium income of just over £500 million from general insurance with a further £350 million from life assurance business. However, in Sir Denis Mountain, Eagle Star had a chairman of Churchillian patriotism, and Allianz's bid was soon described in phrases not unsuited to an invasion.

Within days, however, Sir Denis had found his solution in the form of a rescue by Patrick Sheehy, chairman of BAT Industries. It did not matter that the world's largest private enterprise cigarette manufacturer was an even less likely parent for an insurance group or the awkward truth that if Sheehy had been seriously lining up Eagle Star in his sights for two years, as he said, not a hint had percolated through in any of his public statements. The only thing that mattered was that BAT was British.

Patriotism swept the City. 'Seeing off the Germans' was the order of the day regardless of the cost or the industrial logic. Both these two factors soon disappeared under this wave of patriotism — a development which more than anything else, marked out BAT's bid for Eagle Star as a true symptom of the bid fever by now beginning to reach epidemic proportions.

By the time the Germans withdrew their bid and had taken a cool £163 million profit for their pains, BAT had been forced to pay out £966 million for Eagle Star — a preposterous over-valuation. More worrying, however, were the prospects for the future. BAT's top management made great play of how Eagle Star would form the most suitable 'fourth leg' for which BAT had been searching to place alongside its tobacco, retailing and paper businesses. Quite why a financial services group was so suitable was never explained; until that autumn Sheehy had always publicly suggested that a consumer product group would better serve BAT's skills and needs. In any case BAT's record on diversification was hardly sparkling. In the late 1960s BAT picked cosmetics as its chosen area of expansion, buying Lentheric, Yardley and Germaine Monteil and then turned to the area of retailing, both in the UK and the US. Among other purchases BAT acquired International Stores and the Argos catalogue shops. None of these diversifications outshone the original tobacco business which even in 1982 was still producing three-quarters of group profits.

From Eagle Star's position there was even less logic to the deal. BAT was big; even the bid for Eagle Star could be financed from existing resources without having to go to shareholders for fresh capital. There, however, its suitability as a parent ended for BAT had no experience of the services sector, let alone the very particular problems of financial services. It was obvious from the outset that BAT's attraction for Sir Denis was all negative. Unlike Allianz, Sheehy had promised to leave Eagle Star's management intact to get on by itself. BAT would not interfere; it merely wanted a good dividend each year. It was not the sort of promise which a forward-thinking industrialist should have given. Perhaps, to give him the benefit of the doubt, what Sheehy had promised in truth differed significantly in detail, but that was how it appeared in public.

Whether the bid for Eagle Star mined a hitherto unquarried streak of acquisitiveness in Sheehy, or whether it was just an unusually visible manifestation of an existing vein, Sheehy certainly hit the acquisition trail hard in the following 12 months. The takeovers started with a chain of discount jewellery shops in the High Street, Jewellers Guild. Then BAT increased its stake in the German stores group, Horten, to a controlling 51 per cent. A Portuguese paper business then came under scrutiny, but the next major takeover was in the financial services sector. BAT became the owner of Mark Weinberg's Hambro Life operation when Weinberg and Jacob Rothschild decided that their short-lived engagement for a financial conglomerate wedding should be called off. The transfer to BAT was an amicable one but it still cost Sheehy £664 million to absorb Weinberg.

In the short-term everything looked prosperous at BAT. Pre-tax profits for 1984 rose by 44 per cent to £1.4 billion, topping even ICI for the first time. However by the time Sheehy reported interim figures for 1985 he had only reverses to describe. Profits had declined by 24 per cent in the first half of the year. The shares reacted in similar fashion, falling 43p to 278p and destroying all the previous gains. While currency translations accounted for the worst of the damage, Eagle Star made a poor start under BAT with total profits nearly halving from £70 million to £37 million.

Early in 1986 BAT was forced to admit deep problems in its US retail investments, an earlier diversification hope. More than one-third of its US retail outlets were put up for sale, including the entire chain of Gimbels stores. Next to be sold was Grovewood Securities, the once flourishing industrial investment arm of Eagle Star. After unsuccessful attempts at a management buyout for the whole, Grovewood was dismembered and sold off piecemeal. The bad news on profits continued throughout 1985 with group profits down from the famous £1.4 billion to £1.17 billion at the end of the year. Again Eagle Star had not helped; underwriting losses had increased by £48 million to £174 million. BAT's faith in financial services was kept alive only by a sparkling £50 million first year contribution from Weinberg's business, now renamed Allied Dunbar.

Arbitrageurs

In the first quarter of 1986 the total value of takeover bids reached £2.09 billion. Although this was slightly lower than the figure for the third quarter of 1985, it was more than double the level recorded in the last quarter of 1985. There was no evidence however that bid fever was decreasing. If anything the attack seemed ever more virulent, with predators pumping the market full of high priced paper. Only 16 per cent of the deals were done for cash the remainder were in the bidders' shares or other paper.

Leaving aside the question of whether the flood of paper rather than hard currency represented the final flare up of the fever, the broader picture certainly showed how the attack had been accelerating. Statistics produced by the specialist magazine, *Acquisitions Monthly*, suggest that the value of bids completed in 1985 totalled just over £9 billion whereas the previous year they were only £5.25 billion. In 1983 the figure was an even more modest £2.39 billion, but even that was a jump on the somewhat static annual figures for most of the late 1970s and early 1980s.

Deals were also becoming larger. According to *Acquisitions Monthly*, in 1984 only 10 bids topped the £100 million mark but by 1985 that figure had increased to 23. In the first few weeks of 1986 GEC made a £1.16 billion approach to Plessey, Hanson Trust gatecrashed Imperial's and United Biscuits' £1.2 billion tea party with a £1.9 billion counter offer and Guinness had decided to spoil James Gulliver's attempt to pick up Distillers for £1.8 billion. At the end of 1985 a staggering £10.25 billion worth of bids were pending, several of them of more than £1 billion.

In 1983 when BTR was taking over Tilling and Eagle Star was seeking refuge under BAT's wing those figures were still to come. In the main, people still believed that the level of takeovers represented merely a healthy reflection of the climb out of economic and industrial recession. 'May the best man win' was the philosophy which prevailed as shareholders saw their holdings surge in value with the approach of a predator and increase further still when the high price expected to be paid for control was revealed.

If there were worries they were concentrated on whether the growth in acquisition activity would bring into the UK market some of the nastier practices of Wall Street. Above all the City feared an invasion by Wall Street's arbi-

26

trageurs, the dreaded 'arbs' who pick up strategic share stakes in vulnerable companies, ready to pass them on to the highest bidder for a generous profit.

Ivan Boesky

Of all the Wall Street 'arbs' Ivan Boesky is the most hated and feared, and his shadow briefly overhung the battle for Eagle Star. For a period of weeks over the Christmas of 1983 it seemed as if the tussle for Eagle Star would widen beyond Allianz and BAT. A mystery group of Americans was discovered to own a five per cent stake in Eagle Star and it was possible they would come in with a fresh bid and force Eagle Star to opt between a German or an American parent.

Once the identity of the Americans became known it was clear that a new higher bid could not be expected from this quarter. The stake holders were Boesky and his acquaintances, specialists in passing the parcel. On 6 January it was announced that Eagle Star had picked up the parcel from Boesky, £6.69 million shares of 693.5p each. It was all in a day's trading for Boesky; for the London market it was possibly the biggest matched bargain ever put through. As time went by it became clear however that Wall Street's middlemen were not to make a significant dent in the London market. 'Merger mania', as Boesky was later to call it in the title of his textbook on arbitrage, was as virulent on the American side of the Atlantic. There was more than enough activity at home to keep the arbitrageurs busy on their own patch.

Although most of the arbitrageurs stayed at home British companies still could not afford to rest easy. There were home-grown dealers enough to cause problems, although there were not many identical to Boesky whose kind of professional profit-taking does not seem to have produced many imitators in Britain. However the UK produced its own form of wheeler-dealers who came out of every takeover with a profit whether they appeared on the official scorecard as winner or loser. Others, whose own takeover aims might have been temporarily set back or interrupted, whiled away the pause playing the game of 'pass the parcel' in someone else's takeover. A handful of players brought a rare skill to this pastime and along the way, jacked up share prices generally to ever dizzier heights.

Gerald Ronson

Every City observer has his or her own personal league table of the top wheeler-dealers. Somewhere on each table a place is reserved for Gerald Ronson, the property and motor industry tycoon, whose own status is preserved by the stubbornly unquoted Heron Corporation. Ronson first appeared in this round of financial finessing as early as 1982 when he was involved in bids for Woolworth, the private Littlewoods group, and Associated Communications Corporation (ACC). In all of these bids Ronson failed, as he did eventually the following year when Lord Hanson beat him to UDS.

Out of each apparent disaster Ronson arose smiling and even richer. At Woolworth Ronson toyed briefly with putting together a bid but ultimately left the tired High Street giant to the institutions. At ACC Ronson battled long and hard against Australian tycoon, Robert Holmes à Court, but when he lost he had a tidy little stake to console him. At UDS, the 'pass the parcel' game was carried to new heights. After Ronson had increased his £191 million bid for UDS to £217 million only to see that topped by a £260 million bid by Hanson, Ronson bowed to the inevitable, accepting Hanson shares for his own 10 per cent stake in the company. The swop made him the largest single shareholder in Hanson. It also netted him a stake worth £54 million, double his original investment in UDS.

A further payoff came in the intangible form of Hanson's friendship, an honour not frequently given but, once given, not soon withdrawn. About the same time Ronson's real reward from Woolworth materialized. He became the successful buyer of 32 stores which the company was closing down. As an expert property dealer, Ronson soon had many of them back on the market for a cool £40 million — an 80 per cent profit on his purchase price.

Meanwhile Ronson's mainline property deals were also surging ahead, especially in the US. Probably his prime coup came when he persuaded the executors of the late millionaire recluse, Howard Hughes' estate, to sell him some 1200 acres of Tucson, Arizona. Simply by selling on part of that estate, attractively repackaged, Ronson made a further $150 million. Outsiders soon began to say openly that Ronson's forte was deal making, not outright take-overs, and that wheeling and dealing suited his personality. Though passionately interested in keeping Heron a private corporation, Ronson revels in his public image as a tycoon.

Although Ronson's next major takeover move in the company stakes never even came close to a proper bid he again emerged a winner. This time the target was Tube Investments (TI), the metals and engineering giant, which had fallen to its knees. Early in February 1985 Ronson revealed that he had built up almost a 5 per cent stake in Tubes. Bid rumours about the shares were rife, driving them from just over 200p to around 240p. Two weeks later Ronson deftly withdrew, unloading his shares at what must have been a net 10 per cent profit for a fort-night's investment.

When it came to Burton's fight with the Egyptian Al Fayed family for control of Debenhams in the summer of 1985, Ronson stayed on board to become a kingmaker. Together with Sir Philip Harris, ebullient chief of Harris Queensway, the furniture group, Ronson sat on 8 per cent of Debenhams until the closing hours of the bid. He then handed the department store group over to Burton's Ralph Halpern, by throwing the key stake behind Burton's acceptances.

29

Alan Bond

A British-born Australian probably won himself a place on the list of top finessing by a piece of pure arbitraging in the spring of 1986. Alan Bond, born just outside London in 1938, is now the epitome of the dinkum Aussie. He is burly and direct, his main interest outside brewing lager (both Swan and Castlemaine XXXX, recent acquisitions) is sailing. There too he is phenomenally successful; Bond is the man who brought the America's Cup to Australia in 1983. But his restless energy also bursts forth in the occasional piece of pure dealing. Late in 1985 Thorn EMI, the entertainment and television company, put its entire film industry interests up for sale. Included in the package was a fair amount of British film history, for Thorn EMI Screen Entertainments owned the Elstree Film Studios as well as the ABC cinema chain, Britain's second largest. Screen Entertainments attracted a number of would-be buyers, including the Rank Organisation itself. Thorn EMI hoped to sell to the management, although it was struggling to fund a buyout which would cost at least £100 million.

In December Bond came hurrying up from the Antipodes to save the management buyout. He underwrote their bid while they played for extra time, but to no avail. Although the management team raised an acceptable £110 million to buy the operation, they could not raise the working capital. At the end of March however Bond matched the management's bid (not for him a headache) and won Screen Entertainments himself. That was however just where the game started for within a week Bond had sold Screen Entertainments to the American Cannon Group for £175 million. It was the most elegant and swiftest round of 'pass the parcel' ever seen in the City.

Amongst the fully British contingent of dealers the name of Jacob Rothschild must also loom large. Although a pure City figure — an exile from the family bank, N. M. Rothschild, to be precise — Jacob Rothschild is no Ivan Boesky. Arbitraging is not his prime occupation nor is it even a major interest. When he is not building, destroying and reconstructing his own business (an erratic process which has been going on since 1980), or acting in his formal capacity as a merchant banker, he cannot resist deals.

In Chapter 9 the background to his abortive attempt to build up an instant financial conglomerate, following his ejection from the family bank is set out in more detail. During the 1985 bid battle for Debenhams, Rothschild played a traditional arbitrageur's role. Quite simply he bought in as the battle commenced, banking on the bidders to bale him out by raising the share price by their strife. The deal worked to perfection. While Gerald Ronson played the high profile game of handing a strategic stake to Burton, Rothschild was content to make his profit unsung and virtually unknown.

In the US Jacob Rothschild presents a much higher profile; it is in keeping with the social climate. Hence the highly public foray into financial blackmail (called 'greenmail') with Sir James Goldsmith against St Regis, the paper group. 'Greenmail' is not really feasible in the UK where company law restrictions make it virtually impossible, but in the US predators can buy a stake in a company and threaten the management with a hostile bid. The management is then forced to buy back the same stake at a premium if it is to escape the greenmailer's clutches. St Regis paid the price in order to rid itself of Rothschild and Goldsmith. On other occasions Rothschild appears to be playing either a much longer or a much deeper game than others recognize. Take the case of Tootal, the British textile group which successfully fought off Australia's largest textile combine in 1985. Rothschild built up a 9 per cent stake in Tootal which he used to support the board and see off the Australian group, Entrad. The deal may have been intended as a piece of classic arbitraging. If so, it came off only imperfectly. No other bidder took Entrad's place to continue driving up the shares. On the other hand Tootal's chief executive, Alan Wagstaff, offered a profit forecast handsome enough to keep the shares around the same level as Entrad's bid even after Entrad had gone away. Rothschild, therefore, still had a reasonable profit by the time he sold out the following January.

In any case Rothschild's game plan may never have been bid arbitraging over Tootal. He is also a share dealer pure and simple who enjoys pitting his guesses against the market. If that was his aim then the relatively modest gain from the resilience of Tootal's share price was not only decent enough for a pure investment, it would also have been reinforced by the pleasure of knowing he had anticipated the market in forecasting Tootal's recovery.

It is just possible that Rothschild had set out to play an even longer-term game. As commentators frequently remark, his Rothschild lineage gives him both wealth and impeccable and wide connections. When Tootal's shares failed to top Entrad's price Rothschild may have exited sooner than planned in order not to lose his profit.

Conclusion

As bid fever took hold of the corporate sector few were looking in the right direction for the problems to come. In a market dominated so decisively by the investing institutions, and so tightly controlled by the regulations of the Takeover Code and British company law, arbitrageurs do not flourish nearly so well as in the rough and tumble of Wall Street. In Britain it is the existing institutional shareholders who can hold out until the last moment before accepting a bid, secure in the knowledge that legislation, Stock Exchange rules and the Takeover Code insist that all shareholders receive the best price on offer, even those who are either too idle to accept or are opposed to the offer. If the bid succeeds all shareholders share alike in the gains.

Not even the professionals, at that time, were expressing any concern about the hype which was rapidly gaining momentum. Few bothered to mention the lack of industrial logic in combining Tilling's collection of investments with BTR's. All that mattered was whether Green or Meaney was the management flavour of 1983. With Eagle Star the jingoistic slogans drowned out any analysis of BAT's suitability as an insurance company parent.

It would be quite wrong to write off every takeover since mid-1982 as a symptom of corporate malaise. Many would have been appropriate in a shrewd growth stragegy planned any time in the latter half of the century. Many, also, were the product of much thought and planning; the target company could be expected to provide real synergy when merged with the core businesses. If they did not perform to expectations those acquisitions underlined only the fact that growth is risky and growth by acquisition riskier still.

This latest bout of acquisition madness blinded entrepreneurs to the risks and persuaded them that any price was justified for an acquisition because growth prospects were similarly unlimited. In 1983, it could be argued, those fatal flaws were still forming; share prices were only 60 per cent of what they would reach by 1986. The picture of profit recovery was also only patchy and even those companies which could point to dramatic profits growth in 1982 or 1983 were, in many cases, merely regaining the peaks last scaled in 1978 or 1979. Yet the prices which were beginning to be offered for bid targets suggested that they should show unbroken profits growth for several years to come.

Of even more importance — industrial leaders were distracted from the difficult and slow process of building

33

organic growth by the lure of instant growth by way of takeovers. 'M and A', as the Americans call it, was fast becoming the only game in town by 1983. Only the rarest company could achieve internally the sort of short-term profits surge that could be produced following a major acquisition, where the benefits of merger accounting window-dressing could be exploited to the full.

The trick was to buy something on the point of recovery but just before the board's forecast of it had much credibility. If the recovery were powerful enough, and the wrinkles of merger accounting could be exploited to the full, first year post-acquisition profits could be wonderfully inflated. The next year could take care of itself. Disposal was always an option, on the basis that there were plenty more targets where the original had come from. Meanwhile the general recovery from recession papered over the cracks; after four years of acute recession and some eight years of sluggishness following the 1974 oil crisis even hard-headed businessmen wanted to believe the halcyon days had come at last.

Market professionals, meanwhile, geared themselves up to increased activity. Not for them the headache of worrying if this was the right acquisition. Any deal was grist to the mill of the merchant banker or placing broker so long as the market stayed buoyant. The fatal weaknesses in this attitude were not difficult to detect. Nor was it hard to tell that current professional thinking ran contrary to the most fundamental City principles of objectivity, fairness and long-term commercial health. Health warnings went unheeded as even the professionals made themselves believe that this recovery from recession had recreated British industry in the fast-growth mould of Tokyo or the thrills and spills image of Manhattan.

3

£1 Billion and Beyond

BTR did not manage to win Thomas Tilling until it had increased its bidding to nearly £700 million. BAT had to start at that level and go up to nearly £1 billion before it was able to take over Eagle Star. Between them these two signalled that the era of the megabid had arrived in Britain.

The battles for Tilling and Eagle Star, however, took place within months of each other in 1983. It was not until 1985 that they were topped in terms of size. When they were it was by a clutch of billion-pound bids all launched in the same week which, in total, outstripped the sum of bids for the whole of 1984. With hindsight the strangest thing was that it took so long for the £1 billion record to be breached, considering the momentum of take-over activity at the time. It would be quite wrong to have assumed that the bid for Eagle Star represented some peak of bid fever from which the crisis then abated. On the contrary, when BAT saw off the Germans at the end of 1983 it was just ushering in the first phase of this round of merger mania.

During 1984 bid fever began to rage in earnest through British boardrooms. During 1983 some £2.34 billion was spent on takeovers of public companies. The following year £1.5 billion was committed to bids in one week in December alone. The total at the end of just nine months was £3.62 billion.

A number of factors seemed to be contributing simultaneously. First there was the great bull market in shares. By the end of 1984 the Financial Times Index was impatient to break through the 1000 barrier for the first time ever. Would-be bidders could indulge their acquisitive streaks knowing that the cost could be met by their own high riding shares. At the very least the shares could be pledged against mountains of borrowings.

Secondly, companies were undoubtedly in better shape than they had been for some years. Balance sheets looked healthy: borrowings and stocks were down; reserves were beginning to grow again.

Together these factors stimulated the third and most important cause of the bid fever of the mid-1980s; company chairmen ached to expand. For three or four years they had presided over nothing but retrenchment, rationalization, closures and layoffs. Those who had survived were now seeing the fruits of their labours. Profits were growing again. They seized the chance to expand with both hands.

With emotions running so high it was not surprising that takeovers spiralled. Organic growth could not satisfy nearly fast enough the urge to expand. The need was too urgent to be appeased by normal industrial progress even in the newly balmy climate. The same sense of urgency probably also serves as explanation for why so many takeovers during the period showed little or no industrial logic. This was not a time for the careful addition of complementary businesses. What mattered was how big a mouthful could be swallowed and how quickly.

Occasionally a plum seemed to drop into someone's grasp without any apparent intention or effort at all. That certainly appeared to be the case with the largest takeover of 1984 — that of Hambro Life, the unit linked insurance group. When BAT took over Hambro Life for £664 million, it ranked as the biggest takeover of the year. As discussed further in Chapter 9, the plum, eventually to be renamed Allied Dunbar, toppled in BAT's direction as the grandiose schemes of Jacob Rothschild to form the first financial services conglomerate fell apart within months. To Hambro Life BAT had many of the trappings of a white knight. To the market, in so far as it was an agreed takeover, it was less interesting than many of the smaller but much more bitter tussles.

When Racal, the electronics group, made its £170 million play for locksmiths, Chubb & Son, the victim protested at every opportunity right to the bitter end. Standard Telephone & Cables (STC) encountered much fiercer opposition than it expected when it went for ICL, the British computer group. Despite its own patchy history ICL did not go meekly to the block. Rather it made a great deal of noise, throwing doubt on STC's own rosy forecasts. In view of the way STC plunged into management and orders crises almost immediately afterwards, ICL's gibes began to seem prophetic, if too late for its own independence. Then there was Brooke Bond; the tea group who managed to see off a hostile bid from sugar kings, Tate & Lyle, only by falling to a higher offer from Unilever. This at least was an honourable end to hostilities.

Even the very smallest contests involved the authorities in as much trouble as the multi-million battles. Appeals to the Takeover Panel were a weekly feature of any contested bid. The City Code on anything from the proper use of graphs to the conditions which create a concert party of different individuals acting together as predator had to be constantly sharpened in battles as diverse as the £3 million bid by Gregory Securities for motor dealers, Glanfield Lawrence, and property developer C. H. Beazer's bid for Bath & Portland, one of the blue chip cement and buildings groups.

Dee Corporation

For all the level of activity, however, 1984 was only a warm up session for the following year. In 1985 111 public companies were taken over for a total of no less than £6.4 billion; and at the year end there were another 21 deals outstanding with a face value of a further £10.24 billion, according to *Acquisitions Monthly* magazine.

One of the features which marked both years was the reshaping of the High Street. The stores sector provided probably the most flamboyant and fiery takeovers of both years.

Supermarket operators were also reshuffling their positions in the market share league. The most dashing of newcomers on the supermarkets front was Alec Monk, author of the phenomenal rise of Dee Corporation. Dee had made its first big, although unsuccessful, move in 1982 when it bid for Fitch Lovell, the food group, but was repulsed. Six months later, in 1983, it bought Fitch Lovell's Key Markets chain and Monk was on his way. 1984 saw another major bid — for Booker McConnell. This was halted by a reference to the Monopolies Commission, but Monk was not distracted. While the Booker bid was under the microscope he took the opportunity to buy out one of BAT's unsuccessful diversification attempts, International Stores. *En passant*, he also casually snapped up the 41-strong Lennons chain.

When the Monopolies Commission finally cleared Dee's bid for Booker McConnell, Monk returned to the attack. However, as in the Fitch Lovell battle, he was unsuccessful. By way of consolation, or so it seemed, Monk made his first sortie into the US and came back with Herman's Sporting Goods. Along the way this £272 million bid also made British funding history. It involved the largest ever vendor placing in the London market. Some £330 million of stock was placed, 75 per cent of it with Dee's own shareholders.

By this time Dee ranked eleventh in the league of supermarket chains. As June 1986 opened, Monk modestly announced that he had finessed Dee into third position, by agreeing to buy the somewhat tired Fine Fare supermarket chain from mighty Associated British Foods (ABF). ABF's chairman, the legendary Gary Weston, was apparently too preoccupied with milling and baking to pay sufficient attention to Fine Fare. But even Weston believed in Monk. Part of the £686 million price tag represented 15% of Dee of which ABF became the proud owner.

Monk's purchase of Fine Fare would have attracted attention in its own right; it dramatically reshuffled the High Street league tables; but public attention was diverted from that basic maneouvre by the tactics employed. More than half the Fine Fare deal was financed by means of a £350 million vendor placing, even larger than the one for Herman and only a matter of months later.

By now a number of powerful institutional groups had decided that vendor placings (where investors are chosen by the management whether they are shareholders or not) were not acceptable. They forced Monk's brokers, Rowe & Pitman, the greatest placings firm, to give shareholders a 'clawback right' to 75 per cent of the placing. In effect that meant that the bulk of the placing had been redrawn as an old-fashioned rights issue but with less paper work.

Dee's timing was also unfortunate because the Stock Exchange was at that moment calling for responses to its February discussion paper on shareholders' rights and vendor placings. The institutions dipped their pens in acid to reply although the Exchange had made it clear that it wanted vendor placings to be allowed whatever the dilution to existing shareholders' positions.

By the time Dee had arranged its financing for Fine Fare the UK bid bonanza was in full flood. The £1 billion target had been reached and then nearly doubled in early December 1985. All at once the Australian brewer Elders IXL was making a bid for Allied Lyons, Britain's second largest brewer; Argyll wanted to take over a fiercely hostile Distillers; United Biscuits and Imperial Group were seeking safety in a true merger — and GEC bid for Plessey.

GEC

Throughout 1984, as each successive bid was announced, the same question recurred over and over: Where is GEC? With a cash horde of at least £1.5 billion GEC would not be strained by the size of any conceivable target either at home or abroad. Yet Lord Weinstock, the doyen of British industry and GEC's chief executive, seemed to prefer to hold aloof from the merger mania sweeping other British boardrooms.

As it transpired Lord Weinstock was resistant to the disease but not impervious. By December 1985 he had succumbed to the magpie urge and desperately wanted to collect his old arch competitor, Plessey. In pure commercial terms Weinstock had picked his moment astutely: a number of bear raids had hit Plessey's shares since it had announced a 13 per cent fall in pre-tax profits for the six months to 27 September. Telecommunications were the main trouble. Supplying System X to British Telecom had cost Plessey a sharp drop in profits. The group was also suffering because the fall in oil prices had reduced its Middle Eastern customers' appetites for sophisticated military radio installations.

While not exactly a flea bite at £1.18 billion, the bid did not strain GEC in any financial way. Indeed it was the smallest of the bids launched that December week when £1 billion became yesterday's target. Yet the bid was to cost GEC far more trouble than Weinstock expected, or appeared to expect on 3 December.

In launching the bid GEC adopted what had become almost an old-fashioned approach. Lord Weinstock pleaded industrial logic; the classic benefits of increased scale, cross-fertilization of ideas, rationalization, and concentration of fire power were all invoked. Of course, given the individual sizes of both companies, Lord Weinstock's impressive benefits were all painted against an international backdrop.

That was all very well. Telecommunications is indeed an

international industry in which GEC and Plessey ranked respectively ninth and tenth. But in pursuit of increased international clout GEC could have looked to take over one of its foreign competitors rather than wipe out its only serious competitor in the domestic market. At least that was a sizeable local view. In any case UK competition policy is designed to protect the public good: for which read 'the British public'. Its initial role is to investigate domestic monopolies of which a merged GEC/Plessey would be possibly the most powerful after the nationalized industries.

In less than six weeks the bid had been referred to the Monopolies Commission, an outcome which Weinstock must always have thought probable. At that point the headaches were shared by the Government. Although the bid for Plessey was the smallest of the December batch of megabids, it created most problems for the Government. Quite simply it brought the Conservatives' competition policy into direct conflict with other aspects of its industrial strategy and its defence policies as well.

In particular the Ministry of Defence had been actively seeking rationalization among defence suppliers. With a policy of diversifying supplies on a geographical basis the MOD had already lined up alternative sources abroad and domestic servicers would simply have to take the strain.

GEC also found supporters at Ministerial level in trying for rationalization in the telecommunications supply industry. BT had been continually sniping at GEC and Plessey, and the two private sector suppliers equally regularly complained of BT's procurement policies.

Lord Weinstock played skilfully upon these divergent views in the early stages of the bid. In particular he diplomatically presented the merger as the opportunity to create a truly European electronics group which would be large enough to take on international competition on its own terms.

The rationale sounded persuasive to some. Plessey itself wasted no time in rejecting it out of hand. It countered

41

with a suggestion to buy out GEC's involvement in System X where Plessey firmly believed it was a case of 'too many cooks . . .'. Plessey also had reason to be wary of takeovers. Not three years earlier it had acquired the American telecommunications manufacturer Stromberg-Carlson in a major drive to become truly international. Unfortunately Stromberg-Carlson became instead a loss-making albatross round Plessey's neck.

The battle started off mildly enough, with GEC more keen to stress the benefits to Britain from a giant electronics group than to attack Plessey. But Plessey's chairman, Sir John Clark, for so long identified with the company, soon showed that he had learned some of the tactics of modern corporate warfare. He sued GEC through the US courts on the grounds that it had made an offer to its American shareholders which did not comply with rules laid down by the US Securities and Exchange Commission. He also poured scorn on GEC's track record and invited the Office of Fair Trading to recommend the bid be referred to the Monopolies Commission.

Plessey succeeded in only one of these three ploys. The Delaware courts sent it packing with nothing for its pains. The attack on GEC's performance was always more than a bit over the top. Not only did it not stick but it gave GEC a chance to indulge in a few modern dirty tricks of its own; it sued Plessey for libel.

On 20 January the Government accepted the advice of the Office of Fair Trading and referred the bid to the Monopolies Commission for study. The most immediate effect was that while the battles for Distillers and Imperial raged through the stock market and the newspapers, GEC's attempt to spend most of its cash mountain languished in purdah for most of the rest of the year.

For its opponent the intervening months were of immense benefit. Plessey wasted no time making use of the gift it had been given. Before a fortnight was up it had promoted a junior director, Sir James Blyth, to managing director and heir apparent to Sir John Clark. A Clark had run Plessey for more than 60 years; in its hour of need, the family was prepared to step down in favour of the best man who could be found.

Sir James took up the baton with zest, hurling himself into the counter attack against GEC even though the bid was in limbo during the Monopolies Commission study. He took the opportunity of new orders from the Royal Navy to crow that Plessey had 'busted' GEC's monopoly of naval radar equipment. He relished the announcement of sharply improved nine months' profits.

The shares responded to the twin stimulus of the bid and the defence. They rose by nearly 50 per cent in the three months to the end of February. By the end of April they were floating well above GEC's offer.

Both sides hired high-powered public relations consultants as an integral part of their tactics: Plessey took on Mrs Thatcher's former Press Secretary, Sir Gordon Reece, as special adviser to Sir John. GEC created the new post of Director of Corporate Communications and appointed Philip Connelly, previously PR Director at BP, to the job. It was shrewd thinking by both companies; PR was to become increasingly important in bid battles as the Takeover Panel clamped down on the more overt form of promotion by way of advertisements.

Plessey seemed to have the better of the arguments into the summer. Its unions decided to forget their grievances (at least temporarily) in order to help oppose the bid before the Monopolies Commission. They feared massive redundancies in a rationalization programme. Final quarter profit figures also went Plessey's way pushing total profits up £6.5 million to £170 million during the trough of 1984-5—allowing Sir John to claim that the company was back on course with demonstrable capacity to win sales in the tough international electronics arena.

Some called it playing a straight bat. When presenting

43

the figures Sir John refused even to mention the GEC bid. Behind the scenes it was a different matter; Sir Gordon was earning his fee as special PR adviser. Plessey's shares did not get a major boost from the May profits announcement; but by then the market was going sideways. In any case the damage had already been done. When GEC first made its play it had valued Plessey's shares at 160p. By April they had reached a peak of 246p. Even after the market indigestion of May they were still around 220p. It was clear that GEC's offer would have to increase to over £1.6 billion if it was to be treated seriously.

Bidders commonly have to raise their opening offers significantly before they are successful. It was a feature of the feverish activity of the time that the difference between the sighting shot and the final clincher should be so great. In the case of GEC the opening shot, which had marked the milestone of £1 billion, looked like becoming a £2 billion bid if it was cleared to proceed at all. By early July that decision was still shrouded in mystery, and no clues even about its timing were being leaked from the Monopolies Commission.

Conclusion

By this stage takeover fever had infected so many that the previous bad bout in 1972 had been all but eclipsed. During early summer, however, the market fell into an uneasy slumber, satiated by rights issues or vendor placings, and storing up strength for the next spate of mammoth privatizations.

As the investing institutions rebuilt their cash resources there was time to reflect on the period which most mirrored the mid-80's bid bonanza, 1968. As *The Times* commented in its City pages 1968 saw a spate of mergers as massive in their day as the mega-bids of 1985–6. Schweppes took over Typhoo Tea. National Provincial and Westminster banks chose to merge in what would be the last successful bank merger in modern times. (Lloyds, of course, planned to crack that record by nabbing Standard Chartered but its bid was still running the course at this stage). Viyella bid for English Sewing Cotton, Lucas for Simms Motor, and Bass for William Hancock. Granada took over Robinson Rentals, and Courtaulds topped the hyper-active list with no fewer than three bids.

'It is chilling to note' wrote Kenneth Fleet, *The Times* City Editor, 'that of the bidders in the list, only two — Bass and Granada — have not, in the intervening years, given their shareholders nightmares'.

If these, and similar, thoughts were beginning to chill the blood of investors, it was not apparent among the predators. With the GEC bid still locked in the Monopolies Commission in early June, Dixons was deep into the final phase of its bid, which was just under £2 billion, for Woolworth, and being fought every inch of the way. Lloyds Bank was still in hot pursuit of Standard Chartered; and almost every middle-sized engineering company was either mounting or resisting a bid from one of its competitors.

Moreover the prices at which these bids were pitched reflected the April peak of the bull market. In the grip of bid fever there was no possibility of a downward adjustment to reflect the 10 per cent set back in the market since early spring. It was onwards and upwards at all costs. It was expand or bust. It was 1968 all over again. Somehow it seemed fitting that government ministers should also join the party. Like MacMillan before him in the 1960s, Chancellor Lawson was also proclaiming that: 'we had never had it so good'. In the interests of accuracy, Lawson was forced to admit that this applied only to the 87 per cent of the working population which was holding down a job. For their part the predators and their intended victims behaved as if Lawson was in a position to echo MacMillan's slogan without caveat. Never mind the industrial pitfalls of 13 per cent unemployed, feel the bid price.

4

The Raiders

As recently as mid-1984 the *Financial Times* was still
calling for more companies to be shaken into life by a
takeover threat. It was a matter for regret that bids were
not as common a feature of the London stockmarket as
they were on Wall Street. By the beginning of 1986 the
Financial Times had changed its attitude searching in vain
for industrial logic behind recent takeovers and deploring
the hyper-active tendency of some company chairmen.
Even today there are onlookers of the financial scene who
will hear no evil about industrial predators. Talk is of the
need to plan and invest long term, and the way that
takeovers shorten time horizons so that only immediate
considerations like today's share price counts: they shrug
off such considerations. The long-term is only a string of
short-term moments, they argue. Investment is all about
that string.

The truth is that such onlookers are simply drawn to
the raiders and it is not difficult to see why. To conceive
a takeover bid requires daring and verve and to carry it
through needs careful strategy, skilful tactics and above
all perseverance and determination. Not only are these
characteristics attractive in their own right but, when set
beside the defensive qualities of the targets they seem even
better. Predators may sometimes seem indiscriminate but
they have energy, they aim at growth and believe it is

achievable. Lord Hanson, it could be argued, is not really listened to when he says he always examines the downside risk rather than the upside potential when choosing a takeover victim. To his supporters the rationale matters little. In addition most of the raiding fraternity have powerful and magnetic personalities, usually able to knock out any critical faculties in their staffs and audiences, including the press.

Takeovers certainly have their place in a healthy market. They do not replace the need for good management but with luck transfer assets into the hands of those who will manage them best. That is not, however, the same thing as supporting raiders as an essential element of the marketplace. Raiders are not just those who make a takeover, but those for whom takeovers have become a business in themselves. More often than not this allows little time and less inclination for the unglamorous and deadly slow job of management. Victims of Hanson Trust's bid attacks complain not only of being bruised but have also frequently charged Lord Hanson with buying businesses which he does not understand and does not try to manage with a view to their long-term needs. A former chief executive of London Brick (now renamed Hanson Brick) recently complained that the company was now only a shadow of its former self. In particular he alleged that Hanson had cut prices at the first whiff of weakness in demand, in order to generate short-term returns. James Bristow accused Lord Hanson of greed and squeezing the life out of the golden goose. What Hanson should have done was hold his prices and wait for a market upturn, according to Bristow, who also predicted that Hanson would soon start selling London Brick's assets.

So far that fear is unjustified, although Hanson is certainly a ruthless seller of businesses which do not show a sharp increase in performance in a relatively short time. Hanson argues with conviction that his role in industry is not management, that he invariably leaves to others—but it is acquisitions and no less vital for being so concentrated.

47

Sir Ralph Halpern, the supremely self-confident head of the Burton shops group, simply knows that he is the best retailer around. Every fashion company should yearn to come under his control so far do his ideas outstrip the rest of the High Street. The boards of his competitors could hardly be expected to share this view. What is more surprising is that many investors also remain unconvinced. Burton's takeover of Debenhams in 1985 was far from easy and Halpern's failure so far to inaugurate the much publicized 'galleria' concept in the stores, following his feud with former collaborator, Sir Terence Conran, has added to the number of sceptics.

The market argues that even Sir Owen Green, possibly the only head of an aggressive conglomerate to retain wide acceptability, will one day give ground to a raider in his turn. He may not have achieved much more than Thomas Tilling, the conglomerate he himself raided in 1982. Whatever the weaknesses of the raiders, however, there is no denying their glamour. While investors still fall for glamour (which even insurance company investment managers are likely to do) they will recur in the marketplace.

Sir Ralph Halpern

At regular intervals the High Street becomes a game of musical chairs with the leading groups ending with different owners. Sometimes the effect is minimal; on other occasions there is a major restructuring of retailing patterns. It all seems as essential a part of the constant renewal of the retail industry as the annual changes in fashion. So takeover fever is a much less conspicuous phenomenon in retailing because takeovers are such a common occurrence. Nevertheless, one man has contrived to stand out even in this sector, as the raider all currently fear, mimic and aspire to succeed: Ralph Halpern, chairman and chief executive of the Burton Group.

Ralph Halpern is the very model of the modern mid-

Atlantic businessman from his Burton suits to his professionally colour co-ordinated office, every detail is carefully planned to promote the image. The son of refugees from Vienna who came to Britain in the Thirties, Ralph Halpern epitomises, for many, the days of Austrian couture, now disappeared under the prosaic weight of the Eastern Bloc. Ralph Halpern's interest, however, is in fashion for the masses, even if his concept of the masses extends to shoppers at Harvey Nichols, the classy Knightsbridge department store. When he took over as managing director of the group in 1977 Burton was tailoring 20,000 bespoke suits a week for its gentlemen clientele. Within two years that figure was down to 2,500 and the bulk of Burton's turnover was coming off the peg. Still increasing in importance for sales are the high fashion 'co-ordinated' ranges of clothing for men modelled on the trend in modern womenswear.

Halpern's father had run a thriving textiles business in Austria, but his attempts to repeat this in Britain were not successful. Halpern may give the impression that he somehow inherited Burton, as if by right of succession, but the truth is quite the reverse. He wrested the job from his predecessor, Cyril Spencer, in 1982 in less than amicable circumstances. At that stage Spencer was the uncrowned king of British retailing, responsible for the massive modernization programme at what had been a rather traditional gentlemen's tailors.

During 1982 Spencer began secret negotiations with Gerald Ronson about a possible takeover of Burton by Ronson's private Heron Corporation. After one meeting at which Burton's managing director, Ralph Halpern, was present there was talk of clandestine tape recordings played back by Halpern to the board which revealed that the chairman was prepared to sell out on the cheap. Whatever the truth of these allegations Spencer resigned and Halpern emerged as both chairman and chief executive.

By this time his credentials as a retailer of flair and excitement were unassailable. The lad who had started as a £5 a week trainee shop assistant at Selfridges had spearheaded the Burton's fashion revival at Top Shop, and gone on to sort out the image of Dorothy Perkins, the budget fashion womenswear group acquired by Burton in 1979. Halpern has a weakness for 'buzz' words (indeed for American marketing jargon in general): 'positioning' is one of them. Halpern soon had Perkins 'positioned' as a down market fashion store for young to young middle aged women. More recently he has added sections for their families — 'Little Perks' and 'Baby Perks'. All the ranges, needless to say, are professionally co-ordinated so that mother and baby do not clash in appearance.

Turning round Dorothy Perkins (a process still not completed) proved to be just the beginning. Towards the end of May 1985 Halpern did what his fans had been expecting for many months. He launched a £455 million bid for Debenhams, the department store group. Debenhams had grown slightly down market over the years, but it was still one of the most solid lynchpins of any High Street. Not since 1972, when United Dominion Stores made a determined but unsuccessful attack on it, had anyone dared to bid for Debenhams. Consumers could recite its faults but they still expected to visit Debenhams more often than any other department store.

By the time Halpern emerged as a predator, Debenham's top executives were well alerted to the threat. Weeks before chairman Robert Thornton had said he would head a management buyout of £600 million if it proved necessary to see off marauders. Halpern retorted that he would not be paying anything like 'those sorts of prices' and promptly launched his bid a good 25 per cent below Thornton's threatened defence levels. By the time he had painfully won control of Debenhams in August, however, he had been forced to increase his bid twice and the final level of £560 million was not far from Thornton's figure.

It would be quite unfair to consider Halpern solely as a takeover artist. The acquisitive streak in this leader of middle-of-the-road fashion may be prominent, but he can also grow retail businesses organically. During 1985, for instance, Burton also launched three new separately named ranges within its own empire, aimed at carefully targeted groups of customers less than well served by its existing stores. Principles, Principles for Men and Champions are all flourishing, having hit the mark for clothes for higher paid professional men and women between the ages of 25 and 45, and for sportswear.

Nor is Halpern ignoring tomorrow's development while he searches restlessly for today's takeover. Burton's board is advised, amongst others, by a Futures committee, which includes an anthropologist, a sociologist and an outside design team. Its job is to pick trends which it thinks will be important in future retailing patterns. Already, it seems, it has determined that more women will return to the home in the 1990s bringing a revival of interest in household goods and interior decorating.

Not all Halpern's advisers or collaborators however, stay the course. During the Debenhams battle Halpern made great play of his close friendship with Sir Terence Conran, the interior designer who had embarked on the acquisition trail himself when he merged his Habitat household goods and interior design shops with Selim Zilkha's once fashionable Mothercare group which had begun to lose its way in the late 1970s. Conran, Halpern said, was to have an option over 20 per cent of Debenhams and would be responsible for the redesign of the stores according to the 'galleria' concept of specialist shops-within-shops brought to a fine art in Japan.

That was in August 1985. By February 1986, only six months later, Halpern and his designer friend were at loggerheads. Conran had merged Habitat Mothercare with a third element, British Home Stores, which was having trouble repositioning itself in the market. That move, according to Halpern (never one to mince words), was an affront. Not only did it wipe out Conran's option over a fifth of Debenhams but it meant no design contract. BHS, said Halpern, was a direct High Street competitor.

51

Its owner could not design Debenham's interiors. Conran's view is quite the opposite. He believes his Debenhams options are legally enforceable and battle is brewing between the two men.

Whatever the acrimony from old friends or bested Debenham's directors, for Burton's shareholders the taste was sweet indeed. In the twelve months to September 1985 (before Debenhams) pre-tax profits rose by 42 per cent to £80.2 million on sales of an impressive £551 million. By the following six months that was history. Pre-tax profits for the first half of 1986 had jumped an astonishing 114 per cent to £74.3 million and sales of £620.5 million were a fifth higher than for the whole of the year before. No wonder analysts are looking for profits of £200 million from Burton by 1987.

Top of the tree retailers like Halpern, live by intuition. It is their 'feel' of the market which sets them so dramatically apart from run of the mill operators. Age however begins to tell. At 47 Halpern is at his very fit peak, but just as he seized the crown from Spencer, one day it will be seized from him. When that day comes, Burton may go the way of Debenhams — into the maw of a predator — or the changeover at the top may be by way of internal succession. For the moment Halpern is minding his back by hyperactivity on the takeover front.

Battling for control of Debenhams should have been enough to asborb the energy of any one man yet in the heat of the battle Halpern also found time to take over John Collier, one of Burton's main competitors in the days of old-fashioned traditional menswear. Colliers is now getting the Halpern touch, but to find out why it fell into his clutches one must turn to the greatest British raider of them all: Lord Hanson, the predatory peer.

Lord Hanson

There could hardly be a greater contrast than between Ralph Halpern and James Hanson. Where Halpern is slight and trim, Hanson is immensely tall and rangy. Where Halpern's public image is polished and urbane, each sentence constructed to project the image, Hanson cultivates his reputation as a formidable industrial chief and his conversational style rejects persuasion in favour of steamrolling a listener into his point of view. Halpern courts the media at carefully posed public press conferences and courtly interviews designed to result in personal profiles. Hanson has seen more than his share of newspaper profiles but during takeovers he rarely emerges from his Knightsbridge headquarters for public press meetings. All the overt publicity is directed at shareholders of the target company. City editors however find themselves at the end of streams of off-the-record telephone briefings.

Above all Halpern and Hanson are at opposite poles in their business styles and strategy. Hanson would have nothing to do with the whims of fashion on which Halpern thrives. His much quoted philosophy is to: 'Invest in good quality basic businesses providing essential goods and services'. This interest in unglamorous, low technology sectors, which has stood him in good stead by generating swift and large cash returns, is probably part of the inheritance from his Yorkshire father, who owned a highly profitable road haulage business which was nationalized in 1948. The £3 million compensation ensured that James and brother Bill, if not born with silver spoons in their mouths, certainly qualified as gilded youth. Bill took up show jumping but during the 1950s James Hanson's energies were devoted to society life. An elegant, handsome man-about-town, he was for a year engaged to Audrey Hepburn. But idleness did not keep him in thrall for long.

Before the decade was out Hanson met Gordon (now Sir Gordon) White, another Yorkshire lad who soon became 'more like a twin than a brother' and now runs the US end of the Hanson empire. White and Hanson's first modest foray was a greeting card business in Canada which gave both an undying love for North America where White now lives. Hanson spends up to five months a year across the Atlantic. Business prospered; by 1964 the Hanson company floated on the stockmarket was already a small conglomerate, and since then Hanson's attention has never wavered from it.

In the twenty years since, Hanson Trust has been fuelled by acquisition, although investors have good reason to believe in Hanson's management. It has been in the past three years, however, that it has truly moved into the big league. Earliest of the first division bids was the audacious attack on UDS, the former United Dominion Stores group, also the target of an institutionally-backed bid spear-headed by Gerald Ronson. Hanson won eventually after much bitterness and promptly topped that with a contro-versial programme of selling off many of UDS's businesses, ultimately retaining only the Allders department store chain.

To many people the UDS break up was a simple example of asset stripping, that distasteful predator's pastime last seen in the early 1970s. It certainly helped to make Lord Hanson Britain's most feared predator. Almost any company whose shares began to move mysteriously upwards could believe that the shadow of Lord Hanson hung over them. Enough companies found to their chagrin that Hanson did indeed hang over them and that by 1984 one of the City's favourite guessing games was "What will Hanson do next?"

Hanson wasted no time on tiddlers. The big game in his sights was London Brick, Britain's undisputed market leader in basic building bricks. Hanson began with a massive advertising campaign, a tactic which ultimately earned him a caution from the City authorities in his next takeover battle. He also had a fight on his hands with the Government's competition policy; London Brick's market position gave it true monopoly powers. London Brick's chief executive, Jeremy Rowe, no slouch at financial strategy, appealed to the Monopolies Commission for another study of the bricks market in an attempt to have Hanson's bid ruled out of court. Instead, the Trade

Secretary, then Norman Tebbitt, cleared the predatory peer's approach. The battle was a tough one, however, and Hanson was forced to increase his bid by 25 per cent to £212 million and then again to £247 million. Ultimately, he succeeded only after clever market purchases of shares by Hanson's adviser, Michael Richardson of merchant bankers Rothschild, and when the battle had gone into extra time under the Takeover Code rules.

Hanson's appetite for acquisitions was visibly only whetted by these two takeovers, bruising and lengthy though they had been. Rumours spread that he had his eye on Coats Paton and even Charter Consolidated, part of the metals and industrial interests of the mighty South African Anglo-American combine. First he settled a few American scores by dispensing with US Industries, a diversified holding company whose management was planning a $407 million buyout. Hanson took less than two months (and $571 million) to destroy that dream.

Back in the UK at the end of 1984 he sprang at Powell Duffryn, an engineering group which he reckoned was worth around £150 million. Powell Duffryn, not regarded as one of the great stockmarket stalwarts, saw him off and the bid failed. About the same time, though, the market began to consider the idea that Hanson would some day take over Imperial Group, the world's largest cigarette maker which was also a major snacks producer. The market was right but about 18 months ahead of the event. In the interim Hanson gave the market a jolt by making a £520 million rights issue, second only in size to a £624 million issue by BP in 1981 when it was still half owned by the Government. For light relief about this time Hanson picked up 7 per cent of Bowater, the paper giant, and caused Christopher Hogg, chief executive of the UK's biggest textile group, Courtaulds, several sleepless nights by sniffing around the company.

Hanson's biggest deal in 1985 was on a completely new scale and was again in America. In August Hanson plunged into the middle of what was to have been an easy management buyout of SCM, the old Smith Corona typewriter company and one of Wall Street's dowager duchesses. For the first time Hanson encountered the full battery of strong arm tactics, dirty tricks and appeals to the courts which are commonplace in the US, but hitherto almost unknown in the UK. The SCM manoeuvrings also brought out the scavengers; arbitrageurs like Ivan Boesky who buy into companies which are already big targets as the share price begins its rise. In this case the arbitrageurs bought in at around $66 a share when Hanson and the management were already arguing at around the $72 mark. By offering $73.50 themselves the arbitrageurs forced Hanson up to $75, valuing SCM at a fraction under the magic $1 billion mark. Hanson was battling on several fronts at once. He persuaded the American Securities and Exchange Commission, which rules Wall Street, that the management's funding arrangements with investment house, Merrill Lynch, were improper. He sat out impassively a court case designed to dishonour him by muck raking into 1970s deals between Hanson, White and an Argentine entrepreneur, Peter Bauer-Mengelberg. White described the SCM bid as jungle warfare and as the court hearings dragged on into December it looked as if it was a war Hanson would lose, but Hanson's nerve never once failed him and in January it was rewarded, for he won SCM after one of the most bitter, costly and convoluted battles that even Wall Street had ever seen.

Even before the SCM deal was settled, while some observers were still doubting if Hanson could pull off such an audacious coup in the US, he struck again at home. On December 6 1985, Hanson Trust bid £1.9 billion for Imperial. It was vintage stuff. Although the fans had long been expecting it, the bid was launched just as the rumours had begun to die down. Hanson was, after all, heavily involved elsewhere; not only was the SCM battle still raging, he had increased his Bowater stake to 10 per cent and Coats Paton once more seemed to be attracting him.

Other Hanson hallmarks were also visible. The bid was launched, apparently nonchalantly, late on a Friday evening. There was nothing casual about the timing, however, for Hanson had just produced a set of sparkling figures. All the recent acquisitions had performed well. Pretax profits for the twelve months to September had risen by nearly 50 per cent from £169.1 million to £253 million.

Only Imperial was not thrilled. It already had a merger with United Biscuits in mind. But Hanson's bid overtopped the United Biscuits deal by £700 million or so. The friendly merger had also to overcome a possible objection from the Monopolies Commission. Together Imperial and UB had more than 25 per cent of the snacks market. For the first time US-style bid tactics crossed the Atlantic. Advertising battles brewed in deadly earnest, both sides attacking the other's performance. Libel writs flew. Just before Christmas Imperial's top executives received a hamper from their chairman Geoffrey Kent full of Imperial and UB products. The next day came another present; a brick and an Ever Ready battery (Hanson had also taken over Ever Ready in the early 1980s).

The two friendly camps restructured their deal, promising to sell off a major chunk of their crisp businesses as the price of escaping a Monopolies Commission reference. It was the first time 'refining' had been used as a defence against investigation, but it was soon copied in the other megalithic struggle just emerging for the Distillers Company.

Hanson grimly persevered. He may have successfully argued within his company that a major UK acquisition was necessary to balance SCM in the States. To outsiders it merely looked as if Hanson's acquisitive streak had finally got out of control. Winning Imperial became an obsession. Once the Monopolies Commission let UB back into the game Hanson upped the bid to £2.4 billion. UB matched him. UB's bankers, Morgan Grenfell embarked on a controversial policy of buying their client's shares in order to support the UB share price and thence the value of UB's bid. The Bank of England and the Stock Exchange stepped in to outlaw both this sort of share buying and the by now intolerably boisterous advertising.

Finally UB began to flag, something which never happens to Hanson, a remarkably fit 64-year-old. On April 18 Hanson showed once again that he remains unchallenged as Britain's takeover champion. With Imperial he gained a portfolio of tobacco and brewing interests which, in the true Hanson mould, are declining industries. This time he might have paid too much. Like all Hanson's acquisitions this must produce a phenomenal profits rise under his management to fuel the accelerating growth of Hanson Trust or fetch unusually high prices in a break up auction. It is a formidable challenge.

Sir Owen Green

While some of the leading raiders in this latest epidemic of bid fever have gained reputations for buying anything which came in to view, others are still thought to have kept some notion of selectivity. One such is Sir Owen Green, chairman of the industrial holding company which most rivals Hanson Trust, BTR. Green's successful attack on Thomas Tilling, erstwhile market favourite but by then tiring conglomerate, was an early outrider of the epidemic. In 1984 Green struck again at a much more tired victim, Dunlop. Once again the raid was successful.

Yet company chairmen do not live in fear of Green's tread outside the boardroom door. His shadow does not, as Lord Hanson's does, loom over the whole of British industry. Mostly this is a matter of personality. Hanson is naturally assertive; it is said that when his helicopter approaches Heathrow it is Hanson, like as not, who communicates with the air traffic controllers, not his pilot. Green not only does not follow the cult of the individual, he positively rejects it. During the Tilling battle which proved a cliffhanger up to the eleventh hour, with each side desperately in need of the support of Tilling's institutional shareholders, Green refused personal interviews and only allowed himself to be photographed on one occasion.

Not only is he an intensely private man, Green is one of the few captains of industry who does truly believe credit should be shared among the members of his small top level management team. That is not the same as saying that Green lets his lieutenants step into the limelight in rotation. No one takes a personal curtain call at BTR. The figures are simply published at the due time and analysts may measure the company's performance thereby. This conspicuous absence of razzle dazzle has so far done Green and BTR no harm. The figures have so far spelled out a very healthy performance and suggested the presence of skilled and substantial management.

By a narrow margin Tilling's pension fund and insurance company shareholders opted for BTR's offer. Green's published performance had convinced them of his promise of better management. Whether they will continue indefinitely to be satisfied with figures alone is another matter. Presumably even Green's management will have its difficult times. Some years performance is bound to be flat, if not worse. At that point Green may wish he had spent more time developing relationships with his investors. Too rapid a switch to entertaining shareholders might merely convince them that performance was worse than it was. It must be admitted that, for the present at least, that problem does not appear too urgent.

James Gulliver

When two big cats compete for a kill one of them must lose. It is a lesson which James Gulliver, ebullient Scots chief of the Argyll Group, learnt to his cost in 1986. Until then Gulliver was much admired by the other carnivores of the financial veldt for the ease with which he brought down victims. Presto, Liptons, Hintons were just three of the supermarket groups which had fallen to his clutches. The drinks side of his empire had also grown largely through acquisition and Gulliver was known to be hungry still.

Pre-tax profits for the year to the end of March 1985 grew by 33 per cent to £55.1 million, putting Argyll into the big league not far behind Sainsbury, Tesco and the rest of the supermarket giants. The shares doubled in value and Gulliver became a frequent — and, it must be said, popular — visitor to the stockmarket, detailing his expansion plans and the strategy of putting all the food shops under either the Presto or Lo-cost banners. This was not all Gulliver planned, however, for the time had come for the really big takeover, and there were almost no independent food groups of any size left to acquire. So Gulliver switched his attention to drink, indeed to the grandaddy of drinks companies, the Distillers Company.

Unfortunately Gulliver's first step was a mis-step. Yes, he was interested in Distillers, but not just at the moment, he said at the beginning of September 1985. The Takeover Panel, which regulates City behaviour during bids, took him at his word and imposed a three-month cooling off period before he would be allowed to revive his interest in Distillers. As it turned out, the breathing space not only gave Distillers time to marshall its defences but, fatally for Gulliver, it drew Distillers to the attention of Guinness, the great Anglo-Irish brewing group.

Months earlier Guinness had won a hard-fought battle to take over J. Bell, the Scotch whisky distillers. It would probably have been content to let its Scotch acquisitions rest at that, because the Bell's battle had not been without bruises. The thought that Gulliver might walk off with Distillers, however, was not to be borne. Before they could effectively take over Distillers, however, Guinness had one even greater obstacle to surmount; between them Bell's and Distillers, with its collection of whisky brand names led by Johnny Walker, had a clear dominance of the whisky market. The Monopolies Commission was bound to prevent a tie up between them.

As the battle between Argyll and Guinness rumbled on

after its false start, however, Guinness slowly began to pull ahead because of mistakes by Gulliver. The turning point was probably the revelation about Gulliver's entry in *Who's Who*. For years it had claimed that Gulliver had been to Harvard, but during the course of the bid battle it became clear that the closest he had been to the University was a three-week marketing course at Harvard Business School. Initially Gulliver was able to seize the initiative by complaining about dirty tricks by the other camp. Certainly the information came from the defenders and the City does not like sneaks. As time went by, however, institutions began to feel that maintaining a false entry in *Who's Who* was a more serious offence. Acceptances of Argyll's offer dwindled to a trickle. Ultimately Guinness was the winner though it had to go to full time to achieve victory.

5

The Prey

Everyone knows what a takeover victim looks like: a tired old workhorse which has lost its bounce; a once well piloted ship which has lost its sense of direction; an unquarried mine where the assets are not producing returns. In different hands all these could be revitalized. That is not to say that a change of ownership will recharge them, but it offers hope of a fresh start.

That, at least, is the theory. Certainly in any market there are companies whose values do not compare with their competitors. Not all can be described as undervalued. The market, in its mysterious way, tends to hit the nail on the head. The ponderous call it Efficient Market Theory; practitioners believe in the simple balance between buyers and sellers. When companies under-perform the market it is usually because their investment performance is lagging. Change of ownership is unlikely to be the answer in the majority of cases. There are winners and losers everywhere and no company is guaranteed a permanent winning streak any more than this year's champion jockey can afford to ignore next season's contenders. Market efficiency or no, some companies' potential is under-valued because of temporary under-performance, and generally there will be competitors about who are confident that under their ownership performance will pick up again.

The corollary of the argument that takeover prey can be identified is the theory that good performance protects a company from attack. A business which makes its assets work, continues to increase profits, and shares the success with its shareholders, will, except in rare circumstances, be rewarded by high market recognition. Any would-be predator must be discouraged by the high price he would have to pay to acquire such a treasure. His ownership would add no value. Better to look elsewhere.

Two other factors also generally provide an effective defence; active predatory habits and size. To take the latter first: one of the great motives for growing to be the biggest fish in the pond is that it makes you safe from attack, at least most of the time. Occasionally a smaller fish will show such aggressive qualities that it will challenge even the largest pike in the pond and, very occasionally the small challenger will win, but the argument for size as a defence is a formidable one.

Attack is also a fine form of defence. Some call it the best. Certainly the company which is actively swallowing others generally makes an unpalatable meal itself. This can be partly explained by the risk element. The would-be pedator cannot be sure that his prey has seized upon a digestible morsel himself until digestion is complete. So it behoves an active management without other defences to leave so little time between attacks of its own that its own predators are constantly confused.

Some of the other reasons why active companies are left alone are probably even more emotional. Some theorists call in aid the principle of 'dog does not eat dog'. If a potential target is itself a predator, argues the bigger dog, it probably has sharp enough teeth to put up a good defence as well. Better to prey upon those more obviously less well endowed.

Distillers

For years Distillers (DCL) had looked like a classic case for takeover treatment as an alternative to what seemed like determined suicide. DCL, with its collection of the world's most famous whisky and gin brand names, had frittered away its position as the world's leading Scotch distiller. In the late 1960s it had commanded 60 per cent of the domestic UK whisky market, its top seller, Haig, a runaway leader. By the mid-1980s DCL could call only 20 per cent of the home market its own. Bells was breathing down its neck with an equal overall market share and four or five brands (Bells among them) could claim a 10 per cent personal market share while Haig languished at under 4 per cent.

Abroad it was a similar dismal story. While the Distillers board complained of a shift in drinking habits from brown spirits to white, its share even of a shrinking Scotch export market was dwindling from over 50 per cent to under 30 per cent. Nor did it appear able to capitalize on its clutch of top level gin brands, ranging from Gordons to Tanqueray.

Meanwhile Distillers management continued to treat the company as if it were a listed building like its ornate Robert Adam headquarters in St James's Square. Management control was so decentralized that outsiders found it difficult to establish that a DCL existed at all. Each of the brands had its own board which appeared to owe loyalty only to that product. Group management meetings were like medieval gatherings of the clans—there was no such thing as a Distillers' tartan.

A new chairman, John Connell, was brought in in September 1983, but, even after his appearance, investment in Distillers was a triumph of hope over experience. Earnings per share in 1984 were lower than in 1978. Pre-tax profits had not recovered to the £200 million mark of 1979 and sales had stuck around £1 billion for five years.

Apart from a small acquisition in the US of Somerset,

the American distributors of Johnnie Walker whisky for the past 50 years, nothing seemed to disturb Distillers' calm surface. 'Sleeping giant' was the kindest nickname Distillers attracted. Most others were both more pointed and more vulgar.

Remedial action was urgently needed but Distillers seemed unable to turn its hand to programmes which would be to the purpose. It closed 10 of its 44 distilleries in a bid to contain costs and limit ever growing stocks. That did not seem to produce much immediate benefit, so it closed 10 more. The market saw the second move only as a sign of weakness, both in DCL and Scotch as a drink, and set off a savage retail price war which seemed to hurt Distillers more than any of the other whisky groups. All the while Connell's management seemed stranded with middle range brands at a time when the market at home and abroad had polarized round the de luxe and the discount ends of the industry.

The profit figures for the year to the end of March 1984 were positively dreadful. At the pre-tax level they were a fraction under £192 million and the company was axing a further 715 jobs at two blending and bottling plants in Glasgow, and near Edinburgh at South Queensferry. Against this background, and with Connell predicting only the most general and cautious 'improvement' for the next figures, Distillers' share price began to steam ahead. It had risen steadily since Connell's appointment in the September of 1983 but those hopes had grown thin. What buoyed the shares up continuously from mid-1984 were bid rumours.

For quite some time the names bandied around were North American on the grounds of size more than anything else. By the spring of 1985 Guinness was the name on everyone's lips. It came as a cruel insult therefore, when in the early summer Guinness made its attack on the whisky trade by taking over Bells. What made this the more galling was that at last some sign of recovery was beginning to show at Distillers. John Connell, praised for facing the facts of life, had hauled 1984–5 profits up to £236 million. The slump in American Scotch drinking appeared to have slowed down. A marketing drive had been introduced to reposition the brands at home. Management structures were overhauled and a new managing director, J. W. Holloway brought in.

However, before Connell and his team could taste the fruits of their latest labours the game — as so often at Distillers — had completely changed. In August 1985 self-confident James Gulliver, chairman of the fast-growing Argyll Group, let it be known that he fancied DCL 'but not yet'. It was a mistake from which he did not recover. The City Takeover Panel held him to a three-month cooling off period which allowed Guinness time to digest Bells and come in, if not as a white knight then at least not in such black armour as Gulliver.

If it was bad for Argyll it was the end of the road for Distillers. DCL was still, after all, the country's largest spirits group by far. The bid prices of around £2.5 billion underlined that. At no time, however, was Distillers able to draw the protective mantle of size around itself. Perhaps the most telling symptom of the entire bid battle was that at no stage was it expected that Distillers would survive. So great was the disillusionment with the management that the board's recommendation of the second Guinness offer was not even viewed as much of an advantage. Indeed Guinness laboured under the distinct disadvantage of having to restructure its bid to avoid reference to the Monopolies Commission.

Possibly the ultimate humiliation for the old Distillers' management came in the aftermath of the bid. No sooner had Guinness won success with its £2.7 billion bid than its brokers placed £350 million of Guinness paper, mostly the shares which fell to loser Argyll in return for its Distillers stake. The placing price was only a penny or so below the market price of Guinness's shares. For all the mountain of paper which Guinness had just issued in the course of the bid the market still had an appetite for more.

As his bid sailed through Ernest Saunders, the gritty chief executive of Guinness, must have thought he had reached the finest peak in his career. In fact it soon became clear that he had poisoned his own success. During the bid Saunders had promised to create a new board containing Scottish representatives in honour of Distillers' position. At the head of the whole enlarged group was to be Sir Thomas Risk, Governor of the Bank of Scotland.

Less than three months later Saunders declared that Risk was not to be invited to join the board and that he himself would take over the role of chairman as well as chief executive. Saunders, however, had reckoned without the Takeover Panel which takes a dim view of companies repudiating formal promises made during a bid. By July a major City battle had begun which threatened to spill over into the Department of Trade and Industry.

Tootal

According to the specialist magazine, *Acquisitions Monthly*, only nine of the 139 quoted companies faced with an unwanted bidder in 1985 were successful in seeing off the raider. Few would have rated Tootal's chances of being among that select band, ahead of the £124 million bid from Entrad in February.

Alan Wagstaff, Tootal's 60-year-old chairman and chief executive, is known as a ruthless, if fair, stripper of dead wood. He has had to be. The textile recession of the late 1970s left Tootal in very poor shape. Profits had collapsed to £7.3 million by the year to January 1981. The great investment in the US, American Thread, was returning little despite its position as the leading manufacturer of thread.

Wagstaff set to work with a will. For the end of the 1984–5 year Wagstaff was forecasting powerful recovery to over £20 million when Entrad, Australia's largest textile group, struck. Commentators who had been pleased earlier to credit Wagstaff with masterminding Tootal's recovery, shook their heads over his ability to withstand the Australians. Share prices for the textile sector as a whole stood at around seven times earnings. Entrad's £124 million bid represented a generous ten times the prospective figures. Tootal's recovery was not yet fully consolidated and, as observers remembered vividly, for most of the past five years Tootal had been a sitting duck.

Those days, however, were over. Entrad launched its attack too late. Nearly one-third of Tootal's shareholders baled out into the market in the early days of the bid and Entrad picked up the maximum 29.9 per cent permitted under the Takeover Code by way of market purchases. But the remainder hung on, reinforced at the last moment by Jacob Rothschild, the banker and dealer, who bought a 9 per cent stake.

The Australians withdrew and Wagstaff promised expansion now that the weight of the bid defence had been lifted from the management. Pre-tax profits to January 1985 had been struck at £22.85 million. Throughout the following 12 months Wagstaff forecast an increase to £27 million despite the £1.5 million cost of the bid defence. When it finally came, however, the market's appetite had become jaded by too long expectation and the share price began to fall. Nevertheless Wagstaff could feel pleased with himself. Even after the bid had lapsed Tootal's shares had held up strongly. In December 1985, for instance, Entrad had been able to place its 29.9 per cent at 78p a share compared with its offer price of 72p.

The next test is now looming, however, both for Wagstaff and his supporter Rothschild. True expansion is not easy to produce in businesses as mature as sewing thread, household linens, discount clothing and non-woven wrappings.

Fleet

So far so good. For all its size Distillers is likely to be a suitable case for takeover treatment, though whether

Guinness will achieve the hoped for turnround is another matter. As bid fever took hold of the market, however, basic principles soon faded from predators' memories. All too many of the takeover targets were neither under-valued, badly managed nor promising exceptional recovery in fresh hands.

What, for instance, is one to make of the case of Fleet Holdings, publishers of Express newspapers? The great chain of Beaverbrook newspapers, which epitomized Fleet Street, had fallen to Trafalgar House, the fast growing property and shipping group in 1977. For some years they had been under the joint control of Trafalgar's dynamic duo, Nigel Broackes and Victor Matthews, but the strains began to tell both of the duopoly and of attempting to run newspapers as a mere element of a mixed portfolio of business.

In March 1982 the Express papers, and a collection of magazines published by the Morgan Grampian subsidiary, were floated off from Trafalgar. From the first day there were bid rumours. Some sections of the market even doubted whether Fleet Holdings, the new name for the publishing company, would see out a single week as an independent entity.

They were wrong. Fleet may have been loss-making inside Trafalgar, but singling it out seemed to rejuvenate both Matthews and the business. Far from achieving a modest breakeven in its first nine months to June 1982, Fleet managed profits of nearly £3 million. The City began to speculate on prospects of £4.3 million for the following twelve months.

At the end of 1982 there was a scare when the circulation of the *Daily Express*, once a record beating 4 million, dropped below 2 million but from then on each set of accounts were more encouraging than forecast or guessed at and the shares responded well. By the time of the rights issue in July 1983 they had risen to 89p compared with the flotation price of 22½p. News that the 1982–3 year had produced profits before tax of

£9.5 million, double the earlier hopes, further fuelled the share price. It went to 124p in the September buoyed up by strong profits performance, the intrinsic value of Fleet's 10 per cent stake in Reuters, the news and data information group preparing for public ownership, and a build up in Fleet's shares of a strategic stake by Australian raider, Robert Holmes à Court.

Matthews might insist that Fleet would resist a bid but Holmes à Court had snapped up Associated Communications Corporation, Lord Grade's film and television group, from under the nose of Gerald Ronson, and he was expected to strike again. Continuing news of good profits did nothing to harm the share price throughout the early part of 1984. The Reuters flotation came and went. Suddenly Holmes à Court opted out of the game, 'passing the parcel' (a 10 per cent stake) to printer and publisher Robert Maxwell, who was yearning to own a national newspaper. Still the shares went up. 1983–4 profits had come in at £22.1 million and there were rumours that Maxwell's hopes of buying the Express might meet competition from either 'Tiny' Rowland, the non-Establishment entrepreneur who already owned the *Observer*, or Dr Ashraf Marwan, a former son-in-law of the late Egyptian president, Nasser, and a friend and former business associate of Rowland.

The rumours swirled as Maxwell and Marwan appeared to be settling down to see who could build up the most strategic stake. It was very good news for shareholders. Even when Maxwell bought the *Daily Mirror* in mid-1984 for £110 million, the merry-go-round ride at Fleet swept on. In September Marwan 'passed the parcel', again to Maxwell. The shares climbed higher.

Then, suddenly, everything changed. In January Maxwell bowed to the authorities who forbid the owner of one major newspaper title to buy more. He 'passed the parcel' himself — to United Newspapers, the relatively anonymous publishers of the *Yorkshire Post* and *Punch* magazine. United's chief executive, merchant banker

70

David Stevens, seemed more than happy to pay £30 million for a holding which had cost Maxwell no more than £20 million to acquire. The stake became a springboard for a full bid and the rest is history.

Some critics believe that Stevens may now be regretting having won the Beaverbrook legacy. Certainly he paid a handsome price for something which had three years of profits recovery behind it and which could hardly be said to have escaped the market's closest scrutiny. On fundamentals Fleet was not a natural takeover target by the time United entered the dealing ring. But then would-be newspaper barons have never been totally rational.

Woolworth

The sourest critics of David Steven's attack on Fleet accused him of letting the thrill of the chase blind him to practicalities like price and profits growth potential. The same accusations could not be levied against Stanley Kalms when he launched a massive £1.6 billion bid for F. W. Woolworth in April 1986. Indeed Kalms, the boss of Dixons, the fast moving high street electrical retailer, which had already swallowed up its rival Currys, was busy accusing Woolworth's management of not understanding retailing. 'Not a retailer among them', Kalms sniffed as he went in for the kill. Although superficially Dixon's bid for Woolworth looked in the classic high street mould, however, it was in fact very strange indeed.

Once the most beloved store group in Britain, despite its American origins and parent, Woolies had lost its way completely during the 1970s. Midway through 1981 the 1000 strong chain had to admit that it had slipped for the first time ever into losses in the first half of the year. By the late autumn the problems were acknowledged as the most serious ever faced in its 72-year history. Nothing seemed to go right for the team under new chairman Geoffrey Rodgers. The October closure of the Oxford Street flagship was an all too obvious omen.

71

Exactly a year later Woolworth had disappeared from the ranks of quoted companies, sold to a group of 30 financial institutions for £310 million. The idea, hammered out by Victor Blank, the rising corporate finance star at bankers Charterhouse Japhet, was to nurse the wonder back into Woolworth over a period of seven years. John Beckett, who had just lost a base when S & W Berisford took over British Sugar, became the new Woolworth chairman. The search began for a new chief executive while Beckett ruthlessly began closing whole divisions, such as the Shoppers' World chain.

Under the treatment Woolworth pulled back into profits of £6.1 million for 1982, which was more than the market had expected. The shares rose to a 277p peak on the news, though with the ownership so locked up only a theoretical market existed in the shares.

Despite the recovery there were ominous signs. A chief executive could not be found. One after another the leading High Street talents turned it down. Not even a younger aspirant was prepared to put his future on the line over Woolworth. David Quayle, the DIY wizard, had joined when his B & Q chain fell to Woolworth in 1980. Now he resigned when his experimental 21st Century Shopping store at Bristol was given the thumbs down. His legacy, the B & Q division, flourished with margins of 10 per cent. By contrast the core Woolworth stores could manage only 0.7 per cent.

There were some attempts at positive re-direction. In 1984 Woolworth outbid Harris Queensway with a £177 million bid for Comet, the discount electricals chain which comfortably fitted Woolworth's image. But what made more impact was the continuing saga of store closures. First it was 34 Woolworth core stores, all but two were snapped up by Gerald Ronson. Then Woolworth pulled out of Ireland altogether, selling 18 now empty stores for £7.3 million. The news on the management front was dispiriting: a managing director had been found, but not in the marketplace. Geoffrey Mulcahy had been the finance director.

John Beckett had always said it would take seven years to get Woolies 'turned round, heading in the right direction, accelerating and finally into top gear'. At the end of 1984 he was still grimly reminding the institutions that three full years remained of this cycle. Hope and rumours that Burton's Ralph Halpern was sniffing about, kept the shares bubbling up in the mid 500ps though such levels became merely historic by the beginning of 1985. At that point, when 1984 profits proved to have topped the £50 million mark there was no stopping the shares. From around 525p they soared dizzily to 750p.

At last the profits seemed to be pointing permanently in the right direction — and accelerating. For 1985, for instance, they were £81.3 million. With three parts of his four-part programme complete, Beckett considered that he could hand over the chairmanship. His hand-picked successor was Sir Kenneth Durham, just vacating the hot seat at Unilever but a long-time Woolworth's non-executive director. The old order was changing, with a vengeance. Even Charterhouse Japhet, the merchant bank which masterminded the institutional coup, was squeezed out.

It could be argued that it was a sign of the times that the new merchant bank was Morgan Grenfell, top of the league of takeover advisers. Within a month of Beckett's announcement that he would retire there came the marauding Stanley Kalms with his £1.6 billion bid and the promise to inject true retailing skills. In vain might Beckett complain that the seven year programme was far from complete. His personal decision to retire had made the institutions consider whether they too could afford to retire to the sidelines and take their share profits.

The temptation for the institutions was all too clear. It had taken nearly four years to get Woolworth turned round and moving again. But even £81 million was not a reassuring return from 1000 stores. On the other hand the share price had leapt ahead and once Kalms showed his hand, it surged to 905p. In dealing terms it was time to get out.

For Kalms it should have been a different matter. Naturally he had confidence in his own abilities as a retailer but Woolworth would not be virgin soil waiting for the plough. A wholly new management team was already in there ahead of him and finding the going tough if moderately profitable. The share price too was signalling that Kalms had got his timing wrong. It remained stubbornly above his offer. Most of all, however, as Kalms knew only too well, the price he was being forced to pay, represented a truly remarkable multiple of the future earnings capacity of what would remain essentially an old-fashioned variety store group. In the end his bid failed.

Allied Lyons

If the bid for Woolworth broke one subset of the rules, the attack by Elders IXL, brewer of Foster's lager, Australia's 'amber nectar', on Allied Lyons left few standing. Allied Lyons was not only nearly four times larger than Elders in terms of market value, but its shares had only been re-rated in 1982. It was a highly acquisitive company in its own right and it would cost a fortune to buy. This did not stop Elder's 'dinkum Aussie' chairman, John Elliott.

The recent history of Allied Lyons dates from its 1978 takeover of J. Lyons, the food manufacturer. This highly controversial bid outraged Allied Breweries' shareholders because they had not been consulted in advance. Ultimately it led to a tightening of Stock Exchange rules on large takeovers but Allied continued to leave a sour taste in shareholders' mouths for some years even though it became apparent that Allied had managed to resuscitate Lyons and make it produce worthwhile profits.

By 1983 stockbrokers' analysts were admitting that the turn round had been dramatic and that, in certain periods, the food business was propping up beer sales which frequently suffer cyclical droop. In pursuit of this diversification strength Allied Lyons was out in the market place again, this time spending $10 million on picking up a couple of US ice cream businesses.

Profits responded handsomely. For the twelve months to March 1983, excluding windfalls from property dealing, they rose by 17 per cent. Chairman Sir Derrick Holden Brown, who had taken over after the death of the larger-than-life Sir Keith Showering of the Babycham family, talked of the completion of a three year restructuring programme. The shares responded, as is the way of the stockmarket, by greeting the figures with a 5p drop to 145p.

Allied was not, however, settling back into a peaceful doze again as the market had feared. Britain's second largest brewer went on another shopping spree in February 1984. This time it picked up the drinks interests of Booker McConnell, including the heavily promoted Lamb's Navy Rum and Tia Maria, a popular liqueur. The price of £40 million represented 22 times the acquisitions earnings. Allied was widely said to have paid too much. But it was also admitted that Allied had prised out a superb collection of brand names and doubled its share of the wine market by the deal.

The following month Holden Brown showed that he was still restless. Allied Lyons launched a lager price war to promote its own Skol brand. It also introduced to Britain Australia's other, and some claimed higher selling lager, Castlemaine XXXX. Again profits were rewarding. By the March 1984 year end they were 22 per cent up at £195 million. The market, however, was jaded with this sort of performance from Allied; the shares drifted up only meanly to 162p where the prospective price/earnings multiple was an unexciting 7½ times. While Sir Derrick continued to talk of flexibility, adaptibility and new acquisitions, on top of launching a £10 million expansion programme for the Tetley's beer plant, the shares continued to stagnate into 1985.

In early 1985 the managing director of the brewery side,

Douglas Strachan, resigned unexpectedly, but before the shares could get the shakes he had been replaced from within. A Dutch biscuit manufacturer had also been acquired together with the European rights to Schlitz American beer, and pre-tax profits were unveiled at £219 million. Prospects for lager sales looked good, which pushed the shares up on fundamentals. But something else then occurred which sent them speeding along. Allied became whispered about as a bid target.

The first name to surface was James Hanson, but then hardly a company had not been thought of as a potential victim of the predatory peer. What was more interesting was the speed with which the market hit upon the name of the real predator, Elders of Australia.

At first Elders' moves looked like a complicated ploy to attack its main Australian rivals, Castlemaine. Allied owned a quarter of Castlemaine and Elders initially contented itself with buying a small stake in Allied at a moment when fellow Australian Alan Bond was bidding for half of Castlemaine. Even after Allied had handed its Castlemaine stake over to Bond, Elders continued to build up a presence in the British group.

By September the phony war was over. Elders admitted it was preparing a £1.6 billion bid, although, in recognition of the gulf in size between itself and Allied, it would involve a consortium of Elders' friends. As it turned out Elders' John Elliott was unable to get the consortium off the ground in simple form and pundits began to question whether this failure represented the end of the crazy days of bid fever.

They had reckoned without Elliott's determination. The ace up his sleeve was the backing of the world's largest bank, Citicorp of America. Citicorp was prepared to head a syndicate of international banks which would put up £1.2 billion of the bid price. It was shaping up to be Britain's first multi-billion pound leveraged takeover. Although Elders was offering pure cash, the degree of debt it would have to swallow led market men to gossip about junk bonds and the probability that Elders would have to break up Allied to recoup some of its costs. While the market buzzed Sir Derrick, for Allied, went out and bought a small chain of Scottish hotels. Behind the scenes he was planning even grander counter-attacks.

Meanwhile Elders fell foul, first of the City authorities, and then of the British Government's merger policy. The Takeover Panel insisted that Elder's deal with its banking friends be turned into a pure arms' length banking arrangement; previously the banks had been shareholders or options holders in a new UK company, IXL, set up especially for the takeover. Finally, the Office of Fair Trading decided that a bid for Britain's second largest brewer merited formal examination. The Monopolies Commission is still in the process of studying the bid.

Allied, however, was not leaving its defences to outsiders. In April 1986 Sir Derrick unveiled his very ambitious ploy. Allied had come to an agreement to buy the spirits businesses of Canada's Hiram Walker for £1.25 billion. The brands involved were once again top names and heavily promoted: Kahlua liqueur, Canadian club, Ballantines whisky, and Courvoisier brandy.

This time, however Allied did not have things all its own way. The sale, though agreed with Hiram Walker's board, tempted at least two large Canadian companies into the bidding and the manoeuvrings are still continuing.

Although the final outcome of Elders' bid is not yet clear, what is beyond doubt is the momentum of the current urge to merge. Fundamentals were completely out the window by the autumn of 1985. Those with the acquisitive streak were chasing anything that moved, and the rocketing value of their own shares in the bull market permitted them to contemplate chasing even the fleetest of foot. Between the end of March 1985 and the beginning of April 1986 the Financial Times Index had risen from 956 to 1402 and almost no sector had missed out in the uplift.

Conclusion

What, however, is one to make of the attitude of mind of the top management in some of the more bizarre bids of the past eighteen months? It is one thing to try and take over a flagging operation with prospects of recovery and rejuvenation. But to pay inflated prices for businesses which will never produce more than pedestrian profit growth when their shares have already doubled ahead of the bid?

True signs of mania began to appear early in 1986 when the bidding began to overflow into the engineering and heavy manufacturing sectors. Amongst the metal companies one of the more curious was Mckechnie. Barely had it beaten off a £140 million bid from Williams in February when along came Evered, a hungry industrial mini-conglomerate, with a £161 million bid in April. Mckechnie might be attractive but where did Evered think it would be able to sqeeze out the profits growth needed to justify a price worth 14½ times Mckechnie's forecast 1986 profits of £18 million.

At about the same time another smallish industrial holding company, F. H. Tomkins, was also bent on acquiring another slice of the engineering sector by way of a £175 million bid for Pegler Hattersley. The Tomkins bid had all the hallmarks of opportunism which one might have expected of its chief executive, Greg Hutchings who had come from Hanson Trust. Apart from any other consideration Tomkins was somewhat smaller than Pegler so the bid had to be made entirely by way of Tomkins' shares, at that time flying higher than Pegler's in the market.

It was no wonder that by the end of March 1986 the influential Lex column in the *Financial Times* was unequivocally saying that the market was overheating. At 1400 or so the equities index was indicating a faith in perpetual dividend growth. The accelerating rise in the market was making some people nervous, Lex pronounced in its magisterial way.

The column also noted that the current spate of take-overs had the emotional intensity and ruthless commitment last seen in the late 1960s before the Takeover Panel had been launched to patrol the financial jungle and clean up the undergrowth. Lex was by no means wholly pessimistic at this stage. Perhaps, it mused out loud, the entire market did still warrant re-rating even though it had already surpassed the levels of 1973, just before the property and oil balloons went up. At least this time there was no over-extended banking sector or similar storm cloud gathering.

The last time the cult of the equity had gained adherents, which was in the 1960s, it had rewarded its followers well. This time too it had been fuelled by low gilt yields and by genuine and widespread industrial recovery. But — and it was a big but — the level of takeovers certainly gave rise for concern. 'Decisions made in the heat of the moment, after a few days' analysis, will determine the future of great hunks of British industry', observed the *Financial Times* but would they prove the right decisions for the long term?

6

The Backers

Co-ordination is what makes a bid: get the price right but the timing wrong; the strategy compelling but the tactics fouled up; forget to keep the market either sweet or unsuspecting; fail to sort out the financing — whether by cash, securities or bank loans; muddle the documentation and present it in a form unacceptable to the authorities — all these things will scupper a bid. If one talks to a merchant bank corporate finance department, these are the elements in a takeover for which they are responsible.

In short co-ordination and implementation of strategy. But the honest corporate finance chief would add one more thing — almost certainly more important than anything else — hand holding. Our captains of industry, in the main, have egos as delicate as they are large. Although they are never so happy as when they embark on a titanic takeover struggle, as it progresses they regularly suffer attacks of uncertainty, which only an experienced professional can allay. Such functions are not easily susceptible to analysis, so it is more convenient to pass over what is arguably the most important function — holding the principals' hands during their night terrors — and pass on to the more quantifiable tasks of co-ordination and implementation.

In the takeover of a quoted company the Takeover Panel rules. This entirely voluntary body which administers the equally non-obligatory Code on Mergers and Takeovers (which has come to be called simply, the City Code) has been the most successful bastion and policeman of City morality since its foundation in the early 1970s. Its power owes much to the homogeneity of those over which it attempts to hold sway; the merchant bankers. Woe to the merchant who flouts the principles of the Code and attempts to repeat his offence in a following takeover battle.

That homogeneity is now under threat; some would claim already historic. The 'City Revolution' of which October's 'Big Bang' is the symbol and a major part, has set each merchant house scurrying about looking for a strategy which will both differentiate them from their competitors and give them the lead in the field. Some have opted for asset-management-led operations; some for fashionable securities dealing in an age when debt is said to be moving from bank lending to securitization; others prefer pure banking, or agency dealing — be it stock or insurance broking or estate agency. With each diversification the power of the Bank of England is diminished. Already Jacob Rothschild is described as the 'banker without a bank' because his J. Rothschild Holdings, although acting like a corporate finance department, does not come within a structure which the Bank of England can define as a bank. Moreover Rothschild is not the only individual operating a quasi-banking business but within a structure peculiar to itself alone.

As the differences emerge the Bank of England will find increasing difficulty in imposing its sovereignty. Its offspring, of which the Takeover Panel is the highest achiever, will face corresponding problems. It is possible that the Old Lady of Threadneedle Street (a sobriquet which has not lost all its mystical power even today) retains sufficient liveliness that she can restructure herself to meet this threat. Many old hands in the City are prepared to lay bets that within a handful of years the Securities and Investments Board will look like a Bank of England

81

protégé, rather than the Government-sponsored alternative it was intended to be.

But that is all for the future. The present proffers immense challenges to the Bank's suzerainty, not least in the field of takeovers, and like medieval barons the merchant banks, as her prime subjects, pose the biggest threat of all.

Merchant Bankers

In financial circles the merchant banking houses are the blue bloods, even if their names largely derive from three centuries of Jewish émigrés from Continental persecution. It must be understood that at no time were the British open-armed about their welcome to the immigrants from Leghorn, Amsterdam, the Hanseatic League or the Nordic Alliance. However, for whatever reason these immigrants met less persecution in Britain than they previously had, so their affection for the new land grew proportionately. S. G. Warburg, Hambros, Kleinwort Benson, Schroders, Lazard Brothers, Singer & Friedlander, Ansbacher — just as the names betray their origins despite the rich patina of English county lifestyles, so the origins are constantly revealed in the merchant banker's main asset — fleetness of foot.

Only scratch the surface of one of the blue bloods and you will evoke a red-blooded response. Much respect is paid, for instance, to the sovereignty of the Takeover Panel, until the time comes when the Panel must dish out one of its frequent rebukes. Then the tune changes. Not a merchant house does not believe that its competitors richly deserve their reprimands. Yet, for their own case, a Panel scolding amounts to little more than a bare-faced attempt to stifle proper innovation.

During the battle for Distillers, for example, the arrangement by which Distillers agreed to pay all the expenses of Guinness's bid, was generally regarded as a 'poison pill', a device which would deter other predators.

Morgan Grenfell, the merchant banker to Guinness, does not see it that way at all. By means of highly sophisticated and, dare one say it, doubtful, logic, Morgan Grenfell has proved to its satisfaction that since Distillers would have had to pay its own expenses had it bid for Guinness, it should still shoulder the expenses bill when the roles were reversed.

To be fair to Morgan Grenfell: if its activities have been highlighted more than other banks during this period, that is an indication of its success in corporate finance and not a slur upon its ethics. Under Graham Walsh, head of the Corporate Finance Department since his two-year secondment as Director General of the Takeover Panel in 1979–81, Morgan Grenfell has developed into the leading banker in takeovers, outstripping the previous champion, S. G. Warburg, by 1985.

Morgan cannot be accused of flouting the Code: its principles are jealously upheld. Still there is an element of special pleading in the way the bank now supports the recent crackdown by the Panel on advertising during contested bids. Morgan is delighted that advertising during a battle is now to be restricted to factual information about the advertising company only. Yet it was partly the stirring 'knocking copy' during the Distillers' battle which forced the Panel to act. The Distillers' battle was undoubtedly enlivened by the slanging match which went on between James Gulliver, Argyll's chief, and gritty Ernest Saunders at Guinness. But on more than one occasion the accusations and counter-allegations certainly went way over the top. It is difficult for Morgan to claim that it was responsible for Guinness's successful strategy and tactics and at the same time lay the blame for over-heated advertising solely on the shoulders of what it calls 'unprofessional' public relations and advertising men. It becomes even harder for Morgan to sidestep all responsibility since it made no obvious attempt to distance itself from the advertising campaign until after the Panel had criticized it.

If Morgan has not avoided every peccadillo itself, one of its admirable qualities is it robust attitude to minor faults on its opponent's side. About the same time as Morgan, and Guinness were winning Distillers, it was also acting on the losing side in the contest for Imperial Group, being bankers to United Biscuits whose idea of merging with Imperial was defeated by Hanson Trust. Directors at Morgan who were involved in the struggle of the titans over Imperial, publicly refused any invitation to criticize Hanson or his advisers.

Merchant bankers are little inclined to criticize their opponents after a takeover is finished — a tendency the cynical put down to their awareness that they could as easily be on the opposite side in the next round. They are certainly professional prize fighters and will lay about with all their might for whoever happens to have put up the stake money at the time. But there is more than an element of honour in the concept that many sharp words can be forgiven in the heat of battle which would be contemptible in the aftermath of cool reflection.

One growing tendency the merchant bankers unite to deplore is the resort to law in takeovers. More and more frequently the principals in bid battles turn to the courts for judicial reviews of aspects of bid tactics, or seek judges' permission to slap injunctions on their opponents. Such litigiousness is a commonplace in American takeover battles. Its growing familiarity in Britain is seen as an unwelcome import from the US.

Among recent courtroom bid scenes one of the more interesting was that of Currys v Dixons. Dixons, the fast growing electrical goods retailer, which went on to make a bid to be Britain's largest High Street group by absorbing Woolworth, was then bidding for Currys, another electricals distributor. On the closing day of the bid Dixons claimed victory by a narrow margin. Currys, as might have been expected, demanded a recount. But when that failed to tip the balance Currys went to court. Unfortunately for its defence Lord Justice Vinelot did not over-

throw a significant enough number of Dixon's acceptances, so the bid went through.

So far the courts have been slow to impose the rule of
law in an area both so complex and technical and so
well hedged about with professional regulation from the
Takeover Panel. The merchant banks, however are not
alone in deploring the tendency of legal advisers to attempt
to override the City Code by the courts' authority.

Public opinion of lawyers is never high, especially when
the legal actions they advise for their clients so visibly
swell their own purses. But it ill behoves merchant bankers
to complain about grasping solicitors when their own
'take' in a takeover is even higher. Had Argyll won Distillers, for instance, its total cost would have topped £100
million. In defeat those costs plummeted to under £50
million, mainly because the bankers were prepared to
accept a fee linked to performance. Again the principle is
imported from the US where most lawyers are paid on a
contingency basis: no win, no bill.

What is true is that the high fees earned in takeovers
are very good for banking profits. The profits growth of
the top three merchant houses, as bid fever has raged, tells
its own story.

Growth in Merchant Bank Profits

	1983	1984	1985
Kleinwort Benson	£32.5 m	£44.5 m	£60.3 m (pre-tax)
Morgan Grenfell	N/A	£38.8 m	£54.5 m (pre-tax)
Warburg	£15 m	£18.2 m	£24.9 m (post-tax)

The reason the figures are hard to compare — some being
struck before tax and some after — is that the Bank of

England permits merchant banks to shroud their profits in mystery. If they choose, the banks are free to disclose only their after-tax profits which are reached after a transfer of some portion of trading profits to an inner reserve fund. The Old Lady may argue that such hidden reserves are prudent cushions against lean years. What is apparent is that the practice allows the houses significantly to understate their true profitability.

While the benefits of such cosy practices are only too visible to the public, few realize that in return the merchant houses have voluntarily accepted quite onerous responsibilities. The accepting houses, for instance, that elite club of 16 merchant banks which have special favours from the Bank of England, have pledged themselves to uphold the Takeover Panel. The vigour with which it flourishes 15 years after that pledge was given is a measure of how seriously the promise was meant.

Much criticism is levelled against the merchant banks for the size of the fees they earn in takeovers — one recent City father and a banker himself, claimed that the fees were out of proportion either to the value of the services they represent or the time spent by the bankers in a major bid battle. They are nearly as frequently criticized for the high level of salaries in corporate finance departments. What is never denied is the unusually high calibre of corporate finance specialists. Quite simply these departments in the great merchant houses attract the best brains in the City — and, to be sure, pay accordingly. The practice pays dividends. Merchant bankers live by their wits. Their trade in hand is outwitting the opposing team. Constant innovation is necessary to keep ahead of rivals. Individuals must be the best that money can buy.

There is no doubt that merchant bankers are fully aware of their own excellence. From their pre-eminence they are inclined to condescend to those they regard as lesser members of the City fraternity. Jobbers are usually despised as mere bookmakers, and it is commonplace to hear bankers deride the quality of the institutional fund managers who control the huge assets administered by pension funds, insurance companies and unit trusts. 'Frankly appalling' is how one merchant banker recently dismissed the general run of fund managers.

Whether the institutions live up to their immense responsibilities as shareholders (or are fitted to them) is the subject of a separate chapter, but directors of merchant bank corporate finance departments can certainly feel secure of their superior intellectual agility and quick-wittedness.

Not all of corporate finance work in a bid is flashy manoeuvring or daring market raids. Much more is involved in highly technical and meticulous work behind the scenes. It falls to the merchant banker in most bids to arrange the financing, whether by way of bank or other loans, or the issue of securities. That can entail many months of patient negotiation with other banking professionals; or it can depend on a fine sense of timing if the chosen tactic is the issue of paper in the market. Finally, the merchant banker is the natural choice to head the team of professional advisers. In this capacity he must co-ordinate and support the other members, including lawyers and accountants, over tax planning, document-ation and the like.

As deregulation increases competition and the need for larger and larger amounts of capital, the merchant banks are abandoning independence for the protection of giant conglomerates, one-stop financial supermarkets. As they are absorbed into such multi-function operations so the Bank of England's hegemony is diminished. It may be that the litigiousness of business America, which some say was created by deregulation, will become a regular feature of the British financial sector. If the day comes when the courts can expect to intervene in most bid battles, the Takeover Panel will no longer rule. The financial community may live to regret at least this aspect of the 'City Revolution', for the evidence is certainly mounting that resort to law is on the increase.

Lawyers

Takeovers are one of the very few occasions when lawyers do not hold the centre stage — but they're working on it. At present the leading firms of solicitors which are called in on the bulk of takeovers, concede that the starring role goes to the merchant banker. The increasing complexity of regulation, however, makes the lawyers rub their hands in anticipation. Already the bankers who are advising the principals frequently find it useful to have solicitors as their own personal advisers. Company law, the Financial Services Act, and all that entails for City regulation generally, the proliferating detail in the Takeover Code itself, offer rich pickings for those versed in the thickets of the law.

There is no denying the fact that the increasing tendency of bidders and defenders to seek judicial intervention in recent bids has been fuelled by the self-interest of the principals' legal advisers. The pure City players deplore this, preferring the City's tradition of settling matters by a quick wrestling bout in front of the Panel. Their view, however, is losing ground as outside regulations of various kinds make the game more legalistic in any case.

So far, it must be said, the bouts of courtroom drama have been more vexatious and distracting than serious. Even the legal firms involved see an appeal to law mostly as one of the minor delaying tactics in their battery. Most people would prefer it to stay that way, but the American precedent is worrying. It cannot in fact be long before British businessmen also refuse to stir without a phalanx of legal advisers to bulldoze a path.

While such legalistic tendencies are still more of a threat than a present obstacle, there is still much work for today's legal adviser to do. Acting for the target is quite a different matter from acting for the bidder so it will be best to consider the two functions separately although there are some common elements.

In both cases the legal adviser hopes to have established

a solid relationship with his principal long before the take-over fight breaks out. It is difficult enough to conduct a bid attack or defence without at the same time having to become acquainted with one's own team. The top firms of corporate lawyers spend much time and energy developing a relationship based on familiarity and trust against such contingencies as a future bid. In return they expect to be retained on a permanent basis over many years. Elsewhere in the financial world such long-term relationships are being squeezed in favour of specialists appointed for a particular purpose, paid a single fee, and dismissed when the transaction is over. To date the legal profession has managed to sidestep this tendency. It does occur but much less so than with banking advisers. Where companies feel they need specialist legal advice they tend to hire this in addition to, not instead of, their regular solicitors. Why this should be so is something of a mystery, but it must owe something to the tradition of the Bar whose members have a specialist role quite separate from that of a solicitor. As a result clients do not find it strange to have more than one set of legal advisers; at least not to the extent they would have over a multiplying group of bankers or auditors.

For many of today's megabids do not stop at even two sets of lawyers per side. Dan Mace, a partner in City solicitors, Lovell White & King, and much involved in his firm's takeover activity, says that: 'it is not uncommon for there to be four or five sets dotted about'. While Mace concedes that in most smaller bids there will be just one on each side, he lists a number of reasons why numbers can soar. Sometimes the financial backers or underwriters will want their own advisers. A split board could need two or more; so could a board where one or more members is involved in the bid or a beneficiary under it. Where a concert party exists or may be deemed to, each member of the party may bring his own lawyer along. As the bid progresses shareholders may also add their own advisers to the growing throng.

Lawyers stress that they are part of a working team in which most functions are shared to a greater or lesser extent. Certain tasks fall more naturally to one adviser rather than another. Care of documentation is frequently entrusted to the solicitors in the case. That does not mean the lawyers are responsible for writing most of it. Some of the essential documents fall to auditors and consulting accountants to draw up; others are the strict responsibility of directors. These days professional copy writers and publicists fine tune the material intended for shareholders, the press or for general public consumption. The merchant bank keeps an eye on all these members of the team in order to keep strategy on the rails and tactics co-ordinated.

The lawyer's role as far as documents are concerned lies more with ensuring that they are in a form which will be acceptable to the various authorities. It's a bit like writing to pass a censor. It can be done; professionals do it more easily. They also perform a useful function in acting as a brake on what has been described as 'the hyperbole of the merchant banker and the desperation of the client'. It is also suitable that it should be the lawyer who is responsible for ensuring that all necessary documentation is completed. Not only does their training fit them more for occasions where multitudes of meticulous papers are the order of the day, they may also be free to concentrate on these affairs when the banker or accountant is distracted by market manoeuvres or the preparation of a profit forecast.

Mace insists that the solicitors of the team genuflect as deeply as any of the other members before the City Code, even though their own commercial futures are not so dependent on such piety to a City deity. The piety comes less automatically, however, than it does for the full force of the law. Mace puts it a slightly different way: 'In take-overs we do not have the luxury of being able to bang the table with the law and remind the client that a certain course of action is a criminal offence. Sometimes we advise clients to bend the rules of the Takeover Code and run the risk of a reprimand'.

One might expect merchant bankers to be more circumspect than solicitors when it comes to flouting the Code, but on the whole the score is about even. Lawyers may not need to pay the Code so much attention, but by inclination and training they prefer to act rule book in hand. A merchant banker, by contrast, is a buccaneer by nature. While compliance with the Takeover Code is essential for his survival, the temptation to break a minor rule or two, comes naturally. In the heat of battle no one's blood fires up higher than that of the banker. The recent takeover boom has also undoubtedly increased the merchant bankers' natural tendency towards aggressiveness.

It hardly needs saying that where the law is resorted to in takeovers the lawyers take the lead. Even before US-style litigiousness has quite caught hold over here there are a number of occasions in which the law is already involved. Competition Policy is perhaps the main area of takeover-tailored legislation. Especially when the giants are determined to swallow one another rather than to go fishing for sprats, batteries of lawyers are wheeled out. Once again it will probably be the merchant bank which co-ordinates and leads the team on both strategy and tactics if submissions must be made to the Office of Fair Trading or, in extreme cases, the Monopolies and Mergers Commission. But it will usually be the lawyers who draft the written evidence submitted to those Government bodies.

Among the big City firms of solicitors, two stand head and shoulders above the rest when it comes to takeover activity: Slaughter and May, and Linklaters and Paine. Both are retained to act for the Stock Exchange Council on regular weighty business; both are on the elite list of firms permitted to advise stockbrokers and jobbers. It is a typical chicken and egg conundrum; whether the former work opened doors to takeover business, or the two firms' experience in corporate affairs like takeovers convinced the Stock Exchange of their suitability to enter the inner ranks, the one now certainly reinforces the other.

Five other firms are likely to be on any short list in a major takeover: Clifford Turner, Freshfields, Alan & Overy, Herbert Smith, and Lovell White & King. Partners in each of these firms have been growing visibly sleeker as the recent takeover boom accelerated. All have their tales to tell of shifts in the nature of bid battles, confirming a point made frequently by merchant bankers that each bid breaks new ground, includes some innovation, some twist to an old story or fresh presentation.

One element just creeping into the formalities is the EEC Commission. Most British bids press forward with only the most cursory nod in the direction of the Common Market. Its rules, however, are beginning to have some effect on member States and today's lawyers all have offices in Brussels.

In rare cases British firms may even appeal to Brussels in the hope that within a European-wide market their own clear monopoly in Britain may be thought to be less damaging. The Hanson Trust bid for London Brick involved just such an appeal. In other cases companies with visible monopolies, but in products and services regarded as important to Europe, have hoped to keep their anti-competitive position by an appeal to Europe's best interests viz-à-viz her outside competitors.

Where takeovers stray beyond Europe, into the laws and regulations of foreign countries, British solicitors traditionally hand over to local firms. The law still does not travel well: unlike accountants legal firms are not multinational even these days. English lawyers do not hold themselves out as expert in foreign countries' laws; not even those of Scotland. In return the powerful Law Society takes a very dim view of any foreigner attempting to practice in England without English qualifications. The rules leave the squabbles within Equity, the actors' union, a long way adrift. With the power of the Master of the Rolls behind it, and a membership highly versed in policing procedures as well as their own areas of legal skill, the Law Society's power to repel boarders is a formidable one. British Governments have found to their cost how difficult it is to pass legislation which the Law Society deems to be against its interests. Foreign professionals, however well connected locally, take warning from this precedent.

Attack

Purely domestic takeovers present little less complexity. For the legal adviser to the bidder one of the most formidable obstacles is time. Lawyers on the attacking side are less likely to have had the luxury of a long relationship with their principals. Not only may they have to merge with an infant team — a serious disadvantage — this must be done in secret in the few days and weeks available before news of the intention to bid leaks out.

All the major firms agree that there is far more preparatory work to do on the attacking side. In defence it can be largely a time of nervous inactivity, especially if it is not clear who is waiting to pounce. On the attacking side the contrary can often be the case. The period leading up to the launching of the bid is full of feverish activity; once the bolt is shot, very often, the bidder can do little more than see whether his offer finds favour or not.

Among many items which have featured in the largest and most contested bids of recent years are two important ones: tax planning — a crucial element in Hanson's bid for UDS, because he intended to break it up into its main parts and keep only a selection of the businesses; and formal filings with foreign authorities — a hurdle which unseated Lloyds Bank when it bid for Standard Chartered. Because of Chartered's business in the US through its Union Bank of California, Lloyds was required under American law to register its intent to bid with the Securities and Exchange Commission. Unfortunately it left that process so late in its planning that the US requirement clashed with the Takeover Code's insistence that a bid cannot drag on for more than 60 days. The outcome did not bode well for Lloyds.

More delicate handling is required in financing the bid. The merchant banks, working hand in glove with the principal and sometimes with the principal's clearing bank, or with funding institutions, is responsible for procuring the financing for a bid if that does not come entirely from the company's own internal resources. What can and cannot be done, however, is complex and legalistic. It will be the lawyers who advise on whether a particular financing package complies with all the rules. These range from broad Government-sponsored legislation such as Competition Policy or the provisions of the Companies Acts, to the specifically targeted rules of the Takeover Code by way of the Stock Exchange's restrictions on quoted companies. The Stock Exchange's Yellow Book which details the agreement every company must sign to win a listing, for instance, prohibits a board from buying or selling assets equivalent to more than 25 per cent of its existing capital without prior approval from its shareholders. Following the bids for Distillers and Imperial the exchange tightened that rule to include the purchase of shares during a takeover.

Elders IXL, the Australian brewer which decided to become international with one bound by taking over Allied Lyons, must be wishing that its legal advisers had paid closer attention to the financing package. Elders' chief executive, John Elliott, found his plans stalling for six months because the Monopolies and Mergers Commission deemed it appropriate to examine the role played by a consortium of banks which were to supply most of the £2 billion offer.

More rules hedge about the tactic of market raids — often crucial in providing an early, strategic bridgehead in share terms; and a positive forest now surrounds the key questions of disclosure of holdings or friendly interests. In British law the concept of the 'concert party' — where two or more band together to act with a common cause — was only recognized this decade. Now regulations to police such parties seem to proliferate every year. Most recent is a provision for forcing foreign brokers and agents to reveal the names of their clients when buying shares or face the threat that the holding will be disenfranchised.

Lawyers' claims that their role continually grows and could soon challenge that of the merchant banker as the lead advisory function may only be mild exaggeration. They certainly share a major part of the advisory burden and are increasingly to be found in the second tier also, as advisers to the main line advisers such as the bankers. Probably only the lawyers themselves delight in the prospect of further legalism in takeovers. What is certain is that the tendency undoubtedly favours them. The voluntary nature of the Takeover Code is certainly under threat, both from without as the Government sponsors SIB as the City's quasi-statutory overlord, and from within, as more and more individuals who appear before the Takeover Panel treat it like a court appearance and bring their legal advisers with them.

Brokers

In a takeover, the merchant banker's ultimate value to the principal is that he can dip into his own banking pocket to support his client. The stockbroker's role is arguably more important if he can make shareholders open their pockets — or keep them closed as the need may be.

Certain of the leading stockbrokers are known for this kind of power as others are for their research or agility in dealing. Casenove, arguably the most blue blooded of the stockbrokers, is the only one in the first division not to have signed some alliance with a partner in order to face the challenges of the 'City Revolution'. 'Cas' prefers to go it alone. It is all in keeping with its partnership style over the years; visibly profitable, highly secretive. Some years ago Casenove replaced its partners' nineteenth century desks with modern computer console 'work stations'. A mild-mannered journalist interested in nothing more than the cost of introducing new technology to the City, inquired the cost of each new 'partner's desk'. Scrupulously polite, Casenove accepted the call, but demanded a 10 minute recess to evaluate its reply. When the spokesman returned it was to say: 'On reflection we cannot even confirm that the partners are getting new desks. We are sorry we cannot help you on this matter'.

So consistent is Casenove's secrecy (it runs well beyond what many might consider a natural reluctance to talk to the press) that a standing City witticism runs: 'Casenove has placing power . . . because it says it does'. The rest of the quotation, however, says as much about the stock-broking firm which is regarded as Casenove's greatest rival at the top of the League: Rowe & Pitman: 'R & P has placing power and can be seen to have it'.

For 'placing power' read 'access to investors' and it is instantly clear why such power is essential to a takeover backer. Rowe & Pitman cannot have diminished its power by opting to join the 'Swarm', the City's acronymic nick-name for the financial conglomerate put together by merchant banker S. G. Warburg and including jobbers Akroyd & Smithers, Rowe & Pitman, and the gilts broking specialist Mullens. Officially these four and their specialist subsidiaries come together under Warburg's parent to form Mercury International Group. The City, however, prefers its own nickname which suggests that London now has its own home-grown competitor to America's 'Galloping herd' — the mighty investment house of Merrill Lynch.

Wherever takeovers are rumoured the names of Casenove and Rowe & Pitman cannot be avoided. Between them they feature in at least 50 per cent of all actions, in addition to their predominance in the field of new companies coming to market, whether traditionally or by way of the Government's privatization programme.

Apart from their general contribution to the team, and their unique ability to influence shareholders' decisions about accepting or rejecting a bid, stockbrokers also feature strongly in market raids since they are the only professionals permitted on the stockmarket floor. In any case Rowe & Pitman is held responsible in City gossip for inventing modern 'dawn raids' and the subsequent changes to Stock Exchange rules designed to curtail them.

That was back in the late 1970s when Rowe & Pitman combined with Akroyd to raid the market in shares of Charter Consolidated, picking up the maximum 29.9 per cent stake allowed without triggering off an obligation for an outright bid. As a result the Stock Exchange introduced a ceiling of 15 per cent on the stake which can be picked up in any single raid, and forced a five-day cooling off period. Yet market raids are still a tool in trade of most bids; and Rowe & Pitman is still the leading exponent.

It is not uncommon for takeovers to include two brokers on each side. Frequently both bidder and defender feels the need for a specialist research house to complement market operators like Casenove or Rowe & Pitman. This tendency benefited the erstwhile unknown Scottish firm of Wood Mackenzie, to take but one example. Under its energetic if abrasive senior partner, Johnny Chiene, Wood Mackenzie used its research capacity, first in oils and then pharmaceuticals, to make itself known in the corporate finance sector and hence win a place in most takeovers involving companies in its burgeoning list of research specialities.

Accountants

No advisory team could operate in a takeover without its accountants. Yet curiously, accountants are much less conspicuous in takeovers than either the merchant bank, the solicitors, or even the publicists themselves. Whatever the reason for this low profile it does not mean that good accountants are not vital.

Certain areas of a takeover, by law, must be supervised and authorized by an accountant; any profit forecast, for instance, while the responsibility of the board, must be examined by an accountant to see that it is based on consistent and acceptable assumptions. All financial statements about profits, balance sheets or capital, must be approved by accountants, and of course, any financial results unveiled in the course of a takeover, will have had to be audited.

Accountants, therefore, will generally find themselves busy enough during a bid to warrant special fees in addition to any regular retainer. But their functions may increase still further. The new Financial Services Act which will regulate all prime activities in the City from 1987, lays an extra obligation on auditors to report any suspicions of fraud or misfeasance to SIB and the new City regulatory authorities. The extent of the obligation is still unclear and it will take a number of test cases before the courts before it is known how auditors' relations with clients will be affected. The tendency is the same as for lawyers involved in corporate finance; more court appearances, more statutory responsibilities, more legalism.

Publicists

Professional status is jealously treasured by merchant bankers, lawyers and accountants, and never more so than in a bid context. Each has its professional body to look up to and respect. No wonder, therefore, that the professionals look down upon some members of the advisory team with distaste and contempt. Advertising agencies and public relations firms may lay claim to professional institutions of which they are members. The 'old' professions simply do not admit them.

There is more than a little justification for the professionals' attitude. The PR Institute has not so far established itself as a body able or willing to yoke its members to tough ethical standards. Advertising men believe the intermittent Government rules imposed on them to be 'decent, legal, honest and true' to be more than sufficient constraint. Yet, professional or not, the publicists are at least as important an element in a successful bid or defence as the lawyers and accountants.

However thick the Takeover Code becomes, however constrained by statute and regulation, takeovers will always be rough and tumble commercial fisticuff bouts in which the telling advertisement or carefully dropped public relations hint can be worth the entire set of elegantly drafted offer documents. More bids have succeeded or failed because a City editor listened to a Public Relations man than the professionals will allow themselves to accept.

The power of advertising is more readily conceded but still the professionals have difficulty facing the full extent of the advertising man's influence. Consider these two cases:

(1) The bid for Spillers by Dalgety. Spillers had 45,000 shareholders. Reaching them was only possible by means of advertisements in the national press and on television. The tone of the ad campaign, however, which pleaded with shareholders to resist marauders out to destroy Fred the flour miller, prompted the Takeover Panel to introduce rules limiting hype.

(2) The bid for Imperial. In this bid the advertising campaigns by both Hanson Trust and United Biscuits concentrated on knocking each other's track record, management or prospects. Once again the Panel stepped in, banning 'knocking copy'.

What is most interesting is the timing: the two bids were six years apart, yet before, during and afterwards advertising remained and remains a central feature in takeover. Professional advisers may turn up their noses; the regulators may tighten the screws; publicity has a habit of persisting.

7

The Shareholders

Margaret Thatcher wants to create a nation of share-holders. The Stock Exchange is practising a song and dance routine to welcome the small investor. The Chancellor is even part of the act; in his March 1986 Budget, stamp duty on share buying was halved to 1 per cent. Individuals appear to be responding to the treatment; the numbers who applied for shares when British Telecommunications was floated off by the Government made a nonsense of all the statistics on share ownership. Some 16 per cent of the public, it now appears, may own some shares. Before BT went public the figure had been put at around 8 per cent.

Yet there are few grounds for rejoicing. Compared to that other great share-owning democracy, the USA, the British public has barely begun to dabble in shares. On Wall Street, more than 50 per cent of all companies are controlled by the private investor. In Britain pension funds, insurance companies and unit trusts make up for more than 70 per cent of all quoted securities.

Stock Exchange chairman, Sir Nicholas Goodison, waxes bitter about the government's role in the decline of the individual investor. He describes years of fiscal bias against investors as insurance policies and pension schemes attracted tax concessions while direct share investments attracted only huge surtax levies. In the past eighteen months or so, the Thatcher Administration has gone to considerable efforts to redress the balance. Tax relief on life assurance has gone; pension funds are to be prevented from becoming tax havens for companies' spare cash as their surpluses must be distributed; Personal Equity Plans have been created to attract £2600 a year of individuals' savings into share buying with tax benefits.

Sir Nicholas is right to be bitter. Much could still be done by the Government, and potential investors are still wary of finding tax traps if they venture into the stockmarket. It will also take time to persuade individuals that there is now an alternative to investing through collective schemes or pension funds.

Meanwhile the Stock Exchange itself must shoulder some responsibility for driving away the small investor. Its commission charges have for years been dauntingly high; moreover the new dispensation of negotiated commissions does not look like favouring a gentle flutter either. Commission rates are tumbling for large scale trades but unless the investor is big enough to demand special rates from his broker, it is still expensive for him to deal. The Stock Exchange's commitment to a computerized system of automatic settlement for small bargains holds out firm hopes of cheaper dealing in the future although that is still some time off yet.

It took about 25 years for private shareholders to shrink from controlling 60 per cent of the market to just under 30 per cent. If industry is about to enter a decent period of low inflation and economic growth it may not take nearly so long to woo back individual investors. The BT issue may have been atypical or it may prove to have been the turning point when investors began to come back to the market. It will take at least five years for the picture to come clear, and there will be an election in the middle. Until the private investor does return in large numbers, not even Thatcher's personal distaste for institutionalized savings will prevent the market being dominated by the investing institutions.

Institutions

Biggest by far of the institutional investors is the mighty Prudential which owns just under 4 per cent of Great Britain PLC. Busy turning itself into a general assets manager rather than an insurance company, the Prudential looks after more than £20 billion of funds entrusted to it by policy holders, employees and companies by way of pension schemes, and unit trust holders.

Between them the great company pension funds own about £100 billion of UK equities and this amount may be growing at the rate of £5 billion a year if the funds simply maintain their current split of assets in which UK equities count for just over half. The life assurance companies, taken as a whole, fall only slightly behind the pension funds in the scale of their shareholdings. And the recent bull market has done wonders for the growth of unit trusts, now thought to account for as much as 15 per cent of all shares.

Unit trust groups, which sell directly to the public, are subject to immense pressure from consumers whose criteria for performance are very short term. Many trusts are valued daily and a league table of monthly performance is part of the framework of the industry. Pension funds, which set out to invest contributions today, to provide retirement income in 40 years time, have long-term investment horizons. In recent years, however, they have complained increasingly of pressure to perform in the short term.

A dispassionate observer can see that the short-term performance pressures are actually directed at the investment manager rather than at the pension fund per se. The investment managers either identify themselves so closely with their schemes that they deny the possibility of pressures applying differently, or they find some personal advantage in deliberately confusing themselves with the fund. Outsiders certainly take a more sympathetic approach to complaints that the fund is under undue pressure; investment managers are supposed to be able to resist that kind of thing.

Events of the takeover boom seem to cast doubts on their capacity to resist short-term profits. Studies of the bids launched in 1985 suggest that share prices of target companies shot up an average of 54 per cent ahead of a bid announcement. Leaving aside for a moment the question of what that movement implies in terms of leaks, such share price increases must leave target company shareholders very happy. That includes the institutions which account for 60 per cent or more of most of the larger companies. The only fly in the ointment is the knowledge that the share price will fall back dramatically if the bid fails to materialize.

For this reason, if no other, the institutions have persuaded themselves that it is in the interests of their policy holders or pensioners to maintain the high level share price, and that means encouraging bids. Moreover, once the bid comes, the policy is to hold out for an increase in the offer, which will boost the share price even higher, but then to accept, take the money and run.

The conflict between long-term investment philosophies and the chance to take a short-term profit has intensified as share prices have shot up in a bull market fuelled by the recent string of takeovers. The institutions found it hard enough to reach a decision in 1983 when BTR bid £700 million for Thomas Tilling. Today the stakes are treble that level with a company like Woolworth worth £1.75 billion. For institutions the choice between taking their profits on Woolworth and staying abroad for another three years was even more agonizing.

On the one hand the institutions clearly believed that Woolworth's share price of 775p in mid-May, which represented twenty times earnings, was far too high in real terms. Retailing prospects were simply insufficient to sustain that level; only the bid from Dixons could do that. On that basis the institutions could argue that it was their duty to accept the bid since, if it failed, the shares would sink back to reflect the far from bubbling reality of a hard slog in the High Street. On the other hand, if Dixons believed that Woolworth could produce the level of earnings growth implied by its offer price, the institutions wanted to be around to share in the bonanza.

The institutions' dilemma in takeovers is aggravated by the fact that more often than not these days, they own shares in the bidding company also. That position has its own inbuilt conflict. At current takeover prices most institutions would try to dissuade their executives from mounting bids were it not for a particular consideration: the institutional shareholders are usually the very same institutions called upon to finance the bid, particularly where, as in more than 80 per cent of 1986 bids, the offer is by way of equity not shares.

The lure of underwriting commission fees, or cheap shares purchased at a discount in a placing is hard for most institutions to resist, yet the track record of takeovers in post-war Britain should give them pause to think. Not all takeovers have been failures — far from it. The claims for synergy and industrial logic, however, described in so many offer documents, have proved quite a different matter in practice in so many cases, while the guarantees of spectacular earnings growth have a habit of exploding with some unforeseen economic hiccup. Both of the last two previous bouts of takeover fever, in 1968 and 1972, ended in just such a drizzle of poor profits performance and share price slump.

As the institutions try to decide which line to take in bid battles it is difficult to avoid at least an echo of the merchant bankers' contempt for the calibre of their fund managers. It was certainly true in the past that most pension fund managers were selected from the ranks of faithful low-fliers in the Company Secretary's or Accounts departments. The passed-over Finance Director was a typical choice as investment manager of a pool of assets which was frequently worth more than the company itself. That accusation can no longer be made with such justification; pension fund management is now a financial service in its own right and attracts graduates intent on making it a full-time career right from the start. However, on the whole it still does not attract the same calibre of entrants as the corporate finance departments of the merchant banks.

It could be, therefore, that the investment managers who have to make the takeover decisions for the institutions are simply out of their depth and happy to grab at any profit chance which comes in their way.

While that may be true of some, it can certainly not be said of the men who top the Prudential's investment departments: men like Ron Artus and Mick Newmarch. The Pru makes a virtue out of standing behind good management. It claims to do so even when a bid attack looms and in the main it can substantiate its claim. However there have been notable cases where a degree of Jesuitical sophistry has crept into the Pru's definition of what constitutes 'good' management. The Pru, for instance, was one of the supporters of Geoffrey Kent when he was swept into the hot seat at Imperial Group in 1981. Yet it was more than happy to see Kent ousted in 1986 as Hanson and United fought it out for the tobacco giant.

For the past three or four years the institutions have not needed to worry unduly about whether to bale out in a takeover or stand by to repel boarders. Their investment performance has been good whichever decision they made. A bull market at a time of rapidly falling inflation, has made for real investment returns of around 8 per cent above the rate of inflation. What will happen if the bull market has finally petered out, or if and when inflation starts to rage once more, is something the institutions prefer not to think of for the present. Like companies which can only grow by more and more acquisitions, the institutions are revelling in the takeover boom.

It would be unfair to the institutions, however, not to acknowledge that in many battles their decisions were made for reasons other than the mere cash in hand. When

106

Stanley Kalms of Dixons bid for Currys the institutions gave Kalms his chance to grow big because they believed in his management style. At least, they reckoned it was better than Currys. The management battle argument is too often used as a justification of far more basic urges, but it applied also in the success of Sir Owen Green's takeover of Thomas Tilling. It also explains in part why the ebullient Robert Maxwell, now owner of Mirror Group Newspapers, has such a low hit rate in his all-too-frequent raids. The institutions cannot quite bring themselves to endorse his style of management or financial dealing.

Individuals

If the institutions have been content to share in takeover fever, private shareholders have been going out of their way to catch it. For good reason. As the bid battles rage over their heads they need only sit there powerless but happy as their shares go on up and up. Some commentators have even suggested that the only point they need bear in mind is when to cease holding out and accept an offer. Studies have been undertaken to prove that the best thing a defender can do is reject any initial offer; holding out only increases the value a bidder will put on his prey.

This attitude ignores the long-term implications of takeovers just as much as the institutions' approach. It is also less justified if the offer is being made by way of shares. The private investor offered cash for his holding can usually do what the institution cannot: walk away and find an equivalent company in which to reinvest his gains. Where the offer is by way of paper the private investor has no such let out. In common with his fellow institutional shareholders, if the bid succeeds he will be locked in to take the risk of seeing whether the acquisition produces earnings to match its purchase price.

It is one of the symptoms of takeover fever, however, that such considerations rarely surface. Everyone, from the merchant banker, through the institutions to the small private investor is too busy counting short-term capital gains, corporate finance fees or underwriting commissions to look too far ahead.

Financial Climate

What made all this euphoria was, of course, the bull market. One of the more curious things about the takeover boom was that, once launched, it seemed only to get fresh impetus from any setback in the market's forward surge. Towards the end of April 1986, for instance, the stock market fell back sharply, losing a third of its gain since the beginning of the year. The FT Index, which had topped 1400, fell well below 1300 and continued to point downwards.

Rather than discourage predators, however, this movement positively seemed to encourage them. Lloyds Bank pressed ahead with its bid for Standard Chartered despite the fact that Standard's shares had fallen back to around 800p and Lloyds had insisted that its 750p bid which valued Standard at £1.2 billion had been over-generous when Standard's shares were close on 100p higher.

The rumour machine was also working as hard as ever. Bidders were said to be gathering offstage for Beecham (a regular takeover pointer in any gossip column) and GKN, the engineering giant formerly known proudly as Guest Keen Nettlefolds. Like the rest of the engineering industry GKN had been on its knees during the early 1980s. The first sign of genuine recovery, it was alleged, would have the raiders interested.

Could one detect a note of desperation in the gyrations of the rumour mills? It was difficult to say. British industry could certainly look forward to a period of relative calm and even prosperity though for how long? The share prices of UK companies were still only half those of Wall Street in terms of price/earnings ratios. While City buffs who had been through the bloodbath of 1974 were disbelieving perhaps this generation of entrepreneurs could kick Great Britain PLC back to life. The arguments about whether the market was efficiently predicting this in its takeover activities was hotly debated. Meanwhile the prices which targets were fetching still meant that their new owners had mortgaged the profits until well into the next decade or beyond.

Targeting

While the boom continued what mattered was getting through to the shareholders; putting the message across. It was this burning need which led to the increased use of public relations advisers and advertising campaigns. Ultimately, of course, it led to a sharp cutback in advertising as a result of savage prohibitions imposed by the Takeover Panel. Sometimes it was only the rumour of an advertising campaign that won the day. Early in the bid for Imperial, for instance, Lord Hanson asked the institutional shareholders whether they had noticed Hanson Trust's advertising campaign. It is said that Hanson did not know whether to laugh or cry when told they had indeed taken note. At that point Hanson had not produced a single advertisement. So distasteful did the advertising become that almost everyone was relieved when the Panel cracked down. Some of that relief, though, was tinged with regret. Roger Selig, a corporate finance director of Morgan Grenfell, lamented: 'Advertisements were the best way of getting through to shareholders. They reached the parts official offer documents could not.'

There was another if slightly indirect way, public relations. If the battle for Imperial was an advertising war, one of the hallmarks of the simultaneous struggle for Distillers was the role of PR. Even the most seasoned of journalists were surprised at how assiduously both James Gulliver at Argyll and Guinness's Ernest Saunders cultivated the financial press. Eventually, however, it was Distillers' own publicity machine which topped the other

109

two in practising the black art. Its PR advisers, a City firm called Binns Cornwell, were forced to admit that they had selectively told the financial press about Gulliver's entry in *Who's Who* which incorrectly claimed that he had been to Harvard. The cries of 'foul' which Gulliver set up in response, complicated an already muddled battle almost beyond unravelling.

Rank Organisation

The latest bout of merger mania was not notable for its displays of shareholder assertiveness. Unlike the period in the late 1970s, leading up to the famous attack by Allied Breweries on Lyons, shareholders this time seemed mostly content to take the money and run.

One of the justifications employed by the institutions is that they are more powerful when acting on companies in normal trading conditions rather than in takeovers. It is certainly true that one of the main functions of shareholders/owners is to keep management up to the mark. If an owner is anything, he is the man who can hire and fire the chief executive. In the case of the Rank Organisation in 1983 that was what matters had come to.

For years Sir John Davis had ruled the Rank Organisation as a despot. But as he had aged his effectiveness had waned as his despotism had grown. Rank was in a poor way; only its joint venture with the American Xerox Corporation was keeping it afloat, and even here earnings growth was not what it should be.

By the early 1980s it was clear that shareholders must intervene; but for an interminable length of time the institutions appeared to do nothing. Just as the City was about to pronounce the power of the institutions as lost by their own default, they acted. At Rank's AGM, the Prudential's investment manager who spoke for a group of institutions owning 25 per cent of the shares, stood up and told Sir John that he had reached the end of the road. He was hustled out the back door and away. The hunt was on for a new chief executive. Shareholder power was alive and exercised after all.

About this time Sir Owen Green was battling to absorb the Thomas Tilling collection of companies into BTR. By way of compensation for losing the managing directorship of Tilling, Sir Patrick Meaney was entrusted with the role of finding a new chief executive for Rank. At that point things began to go wrong. Sir Patrick came up with no one. After several months the institutions called it a stalemate, Sir Patrick stepped into the position himself, and Michael Gifford came in as a managing director under him.

To some the institutions' moves over Rank were a cynical display of self-interest and indifference to their real responsibilities. Sir Patrick Meaney was godfather of one of the children of Ron Artus, the investment chief of the Prudential. To others the mixed outcome of the institutions' intervention at Rank was just a symptom of how difficult such shareholder responsibilities are to perform.

The case of Rank was almost the last time institutions exercised shareholder power — at least publicly. Perhaps their seeming connivance at the most opportunistic of takeovers in the next few years was more a reflection of their bruises from the Rank affair than a laissez faire attitude to takeovers.

8

Tactics

For reasons which have much to do with the high level of takeover activity, more and more top executives are finding themselves owners of their companies these days rather than just managers. Management buyouts have now become a sophisticated financial ploy often used as a complement or alternative to a takeover. A bidder, for instance, may make an arrangement with the management of peripheral parts of the target in his sights to sell them those aspects of the business that he does not want to retain. He reduces his takeover costs and the burden of twisting profits out of recalcitrant or unfamiliar products. They get the chance to run the businesses they know best. In that way management buyouts frequently complement a takeover. Because they are looked upon with favour the predator who takes over a large group and sells part of it off to its management, is seldom accused of asset stripping, an allegation which springs rapidly to the lips of critics when any other kind of break up is planned.

Management Buyouts

Haden, a medium-sized company in the engineering sector, was probably the first to use the management buyout as a defence in a contested bid. Its executives put together a £56 million bid for the company which easily outstripped the £33 million unwelcome attack which had been made by Trafalgar House. It was said at the time that only the managers could have known enough about the business to have dared put in such a high bid. They were certainly proved right. Not long afterwards Haden revealed that BICC had made an offer for its UK operations which would nearly pay for redeeming the great mountain of convertible preference shares which supporters of the buyout had subscribed for. Everyone, it seemed, but Trafalgar House, came out with a gain; and the beauty of it is that no one carps about 'insider information' in such circumstances.

While the buyout at Haden was made in the face of an unwelcome bid for the whole company, more typical are those made for parts of a business which have attracted snoopers. Chairmen of large organizations with untidy corners which are attractive to outsiders simply feel more comfortable selling to the management. Besides, it looks better in the City. It speaks volumes for the degree to which management buyouts have become an ordinary fixture in the corporate finance emporium that managers no longer expect to buy their operations at deep discounts to the open market price. If there is another bidder about, the management must at least match any opening bid in order to have a chance of success.

It was not always so. Management buyouts first emerged during the recession of the early 1980s. Then they were a way for top boards to sell off unwanted parts of the business to those who could possibly make them work harder by being more directly involved. Management buyouts, in short, were an alternative to full-scale de-mergers of giant corporations. To some extent they still are, since the promise of de-mergers which looked so bright in the early days of the Thatcher administration, has all but gone out.

Those early days for buyouts also coincided with savage industrial recession. Boards were so keen to be rid of flagging offshoots that price was a secondary consideration. The first management buyouts were typicaly done on the cheap although the management themselves could frequently judge with precision how much profits would leap back once the dead hand of a giant combine was lifted from them.

Times change. The recession began to lift; public company boards began to see how profitable buyouts could be; in City terms they became even commonplace. The result was a gradual rise in the value placed on the assets to be spun off. In 1985, for instance, when Rank decided to sell off some leisure interests, the management was required to match at least one outside bid. Not all management buyouts come off. Witness the attempted buyout of Screen Entertainments from Thorn EMI at the tail end of 1985. The management narrowly failed to raise all the essential capital and Screen Entertainments ended up with the US film group, Cannon, after a one-week sojourn in the pocket of Australia's Alan Bond who had earlier featured briefly as the management's supporter.

Most failed management buyouts do not end up as the counter in a game of financial 'pass the parcel' as Screen Entertainments did. Nor do they take place, like Haden, in the context of an unwelcome bid. Sufficient numbers of them, however, have occurred as a result of, or in place of takeovers, that it is now standard practice for any company vulnerable to a bid to consider buyouts as an alternative to being taken over.

Poison Pills

An even more classic defensive tactic in the face of a possible takeover is to swallow what the Americans have nicknamed the 'poison pill', something which would make an attacker very sick indeed if he tried to lunch off the poisoned bait.

Chapter 6 discussed how merchant bankers, Morgan Grenfell, reacted to claims that Distillers and Guinness had contrived a 'poison pill' when Distillers agreed to pay

Guinness's costs in taking them over. Although 'poison pills' are common across the Atlantic, British companies seem to find them a distasteful concept. Morgan Grenfell is not the only one to deny employing corporate pesticides. In its attempt to see off what it regarded as an impudent bid from the Australian brewer, Elders, Allied Lyons chose a traditional defence. It obtained shareholders' approval to mount a £1.25 billion bid of its own — for the spirits business of Canada's Hiram Walker. To outsiders this was determined 'poison pill' tactics: at a stroke it would make Allied both unpalatable and too big a mouthful for Elders. Allied's board insisted that the acquisition had been long in the planning. They indignantly denied that it constituted little but hasty pill swallowing.

Examples of 'poison pills' being used on this side of the Atlantic are rare. If a pill is to be effective in scaring away a determined predator it must be powerful medicine. But Stock Exchange and Takeover Code rules combine to outlaw most forms of medicine strong enough to do the trick.

In the first place companies are strictly limited in what they may do to change the shape of the business once a takeover is heralded. The defender may not try to make itself unattractive by selling the assets for which the bidder is willing to pay.

This rule merely reinforces the general Stock Exchange restriction (which applies at all times, not just when take-overs loom) on a board's freedom to alter the shape of a company. Ever since 1978 when Allied Breweries planned to takeover Lyons by way of a routine board decision the Stock Exchange has insisted that shareholders must give prior approval to any purchase or sale of assets amounting to more than a quarter of the company's existing asset base. Thus, eight years later, when Allied Lyons wanted to grow big enough to deter Elders, it sought shareholders' agreement to the £1.25 billion purchase of Hiram Walker.

In Allied Lyons' case the board was successful in looking for shareholders' permission to go out on such a lavish shopping spree; but it is a high risk manoeuvre. Many company chairmen have found to their chagrin that shareholders will not permit major diversifications from core businesses by means of large purchases or disposals. Yet if an asset sale or purchase is to be an effective 'poison pill' it must be of a significant size. Although the Distillers–Guinness agreement over takeover costs shows that 'poison pill' plans are still laid and can be effective, British rules generally prevent the most common sort of pill.

Greenmail

The peculiarities of British rules are also credited with the absence of 'greenmail' in British corporate struggles. In the US it is nearly as common as takeovers themselves. Many professional Wall Street arbitrageurs specialize in the practice. Usually the arbitrageur builds up a shareholding just large enough to form a credible springboard for a hostile bid. A rattled board can be persuaded that the only way to prevent the bid is to buy out the holding at whatever price the predator demands. A classic case of blackmail which is nicknamed a different colour on the grounds of the number of dollar bills involved.

British companies can almost never pay out so the arbitrageur or deal maker rarely has an incentive to turn greenmailer. Until recently British company law forbad companies to buy their own shares. In the early 1980s that blanket prohibition was relaxed and companies may now buy in shares under certain circumstances but only in order to cancel them. Cancellation, by reducing the equity base, enhances the capital value of all shareholders equally. This is of little interest to the would-be greenmailer.

Nonetheless rumours of 'greenmail' or 'greenmail averted' persist in the City. One particularly intriguing variation being a case where 'greenmail' was to have been turned against the greenmailer by means of a takeover by the original planned victim. In the event neither the greenmailing nor the role reversal took place but the prospect that both might have occurred kept the City entertained for months during the winter and spring of 1985–6.

This rumour centred on Stock Conversion, an elderly property company of considerable charm to the thrusting young developer, Stockley, which pined for Conversion's established estates. Stockley built up a large 26.6 per cent stake in Stock Conversion and was widely expected to make an outright bid. At the last moment, however, Stockley veered away, and Stock Conversion sank gratefully into the arms of P & O whose property tycoon chairman, Jeffrey Stirling, proposed an agreed bid.

Prior to that happy event, according to the rumour, Stock Conversion had planned to defeat Stockley, not by paying it to go away but by smothering it. Stock Conversion was larger than Stockley. It therefore proposed to turn raider itself and launch a counterbid on the upstart. This would, of course, have the same effect as paying off a blackmailer; it would cancel the unfriendly shareholding. It would, moreover, do so by way of a positive strategy which would reward Stock Conversion with Stockley's development drive and energy. A second bird could also be brought down. Over the years the City had come to view Stock Conversion as tired rather than merely long-established. By turning the tables on Stockley, Stock Conversion would revitalize its own image.

Whatever the realities of the interplay between the three companies, the City amused itself for several happy months believing that Stock Conversion had planned to annihilate a greenmailer by absorption rather than rejection. When Stock Conversion instead chose to seek protection under P & O's umbrella, the jollity evaporated. City critics then reminded themselves that they had earlier recognized symptoms of decline in Stock Conversion.

117

Libel

According to the lawyers the torrents of libel writs which accompany modern contested bids should be regarded as diversionary tactics. Certainly there seemed a curious lack of conviction about those that arose during the Distillers–Argyll affair. Lawyers do not always rule their clients completely, any more than merchant banks do. Captains of industry do not give up all their independence when they seek professional advice in a takeover battle. There are numerous occasions when the advisers' views are overruled and the policy or tactic adopted unmistakably reflects the persona of the principal himself.

It is hard to avoid such thoughts when mulling over GEC's decision to sue Plessey for libel on the grounds that its defence document contained 'a caricature' of GEC and a 'fanciful idealization' of itself. In the past most companies would have been content to report any aspect of a document they disliked to the Takeover Panel. If necessary the Panel would have demanded a redrafting or retraction and there the matter would have ended.

That was simply not enough for Lord Weinstock, GEC's chief executive and on some accounts Britain's top industrialist. The 'Blessed Arnold' (as Lord Weinstock is known in the City) was stung to the quick by Plessey's jibes. Outsiders might advise that with the bid on ice for at least six months while it was studied by the Monopolies Commission, Weinstock would do better to leave well alone. Lord Weinstock would have none of that. He burned for revenge. Only the courts could give him this in ample measure.

Lord Weinstock's injured feelings, however, form only one thread in the increasingly legalistic tangle into which British takeovers have fallen. Whatever the Government may claim about the clarity of its Monopolies Policy, and the City for the speed and flexibility of self regulation, companies are clearly looking for greater certainty and authority in this delicate area. If Government will neither

118

rewrite its policy to give a lead nor turn voluntary City watchdogs into real policemen, then companies will go to the clearest authority they can find: the courts.

It is a message which has been coming across increasingly loudly. Whether it is Rank demanding that the courts decide if the Independent Broadcasting Authority had power to thwart its bid for Granada Television, or Argyll seeking to overturn the Office of Fair Trading's ruling that Guinness could bid for Distillers, certainty is all.

Government does not seem to be heeding this plea from the business community but Parliament, by a strange irony, is showing signs of listening. The travails of the Financial Services Bill (designed to provide the regulatory framework for the City after the 'Big Bang') have seen Parliament insist that the key watchdogs — the Securities and Investments Board (SIB) and the subordinate Self Regulatory Organizations (SRO) — should be given at least some statutory trappings.

SIB has now been named in the legislation as the top power in the City; it and the SROs have gained immunity against prosecution. The regulatory structure is getting much closer to a fullscale statutory system than ever Government wanted or planned. At present the Takeover Panel remains outside these tendencies: as the new structures were being devised it pointedly chose to remain a voluntary body. Yet the trend is so strong that it can be only a matter of time before the Panel too is given some statutory powers. When, and if, that occurs, many of the appeals to the general courts in takeover battles should cease.

Professionals

Since merchant banks are generally in charge of strategy and its implementation during bid battles, it is not surprising that they are usually implicated in any controversial new tactic which comes to be employed. Indeed the merchant bankers rank themselves mainly on their

119

ability to outwit other bankers' tactics and dream up effective counter-measures of their own.

Some of the so-called 'new inventions', however, are actually just variations on old themes. During the spate of mega-bids in 1986, for example, Morgan Grenfell won notoriety for buying large numbers of Distillers' shares for Guinness, its client. A week earlier it had done the same for United Biscuits, namely, bought heavily into Imperial. Total cost of the purchases by Morgan was said to be about £550 million. Morgan's own shareholders' funds stood at only £174 million. The risk involved in such an imbalance alarmed the Bank of England. In early March it ruled that banks could not support clients' strategies by buying shares worth more than 25 per cent of the banks' own capital. The Stock Exchange took the same opportunity to tighten its rules so that companies could not lightly give out indemnities against advisers' losses on such share deals.

For those with long memories the share buying tactics and the new curbs on them recalled the epic battle between Dalgety and Spillers in the late 1970s. Then merchant bankers, Lazards, was forced to convince the Takeover Panel that it had been buying Spillers' shares at its own risk and would not be indemnified by Spillers, who happened to be its client.

Morgan Grenfell's claim to originality in another feature of the Guinness bid is more sustainable: its representation to the Monopolies Commission. Guinness was originally ruled out from bidding for Distillers because, having just acquired Bells whisky, it would end up with far too much of the Scotch whisky market. Morgan came to a deal with the Office of Fair Trading: Guinness would agree to sell to Lonrho ten whisky brands, so bringing its own future share of the total market down to the key 25 per cent mark.

The tactic worked; Guinness was permitted to make its eventually successful bid, and Morgan could claim a first in persuading the Monopolies Commission that a predator could represent his case if sufficient alterations had been made to it. Morgan had, in fact, been working up to this point during the battle for Imperial. In that case it had won permission from the Commission for Imperial and United Biscuits to swop sides. The prohibited predator became a permitted target after promises to dispose of a too-bulky crisps business.

Like many takeover tactics, however, the Guinness manoeuvre of selling off brands was a two-edged weapon. Barely had the takeover been successfully won when Guinness found itself in trouble with its shareholders at the annual meeting in May. Their complaint was that brands as important as these must surely be worth more than Lonrho was being asked to pay. Guinness was selling them too cheap.

When it comes to the 'dirty tricks' department it is hard to avoid the conclusion that the merchant bankers, so agile in inventing tactics, must also be involved. But so far no evidence points firmly at them alone. Yet 'dirty tricks' do seem to be on the increase.

Advertising became so aggressive during the spring bids of 1986 that the authorities were forced to impose savage restrictions, another throwback to the Spillers–Dalgety battle when Fred, Spillers' 'Flour Man', appeared above highly charged copy in every national newspaper.

Around the same time there was much talk about private investigators being used to discredit opponents. Raymond Miquel, chairman of Bells, complained that private investigators were prying into his private life during the takeover by Guinness. James Gulliver, head of Argyll, won much early mileage out of pinpointing Distillers as the source of leaks about his misleading entry in *Who's Who*. Later, Gulliver himself came under attack for placing the entry in the publication. David Connell, brother of the Distillers' chairman and himself head of the Johnny Walker brand, was burgled in mysterious circumstances during the bid. Almost nothing of value was stolen. Distillers itself feared industrial espionage or simple spying

121

so deeply that it had its boardroom checked for bugs each day.

By Wall Street standards British bids are still fought largely free from 'dirty tricks', but they have been creeping in. Participants in this latest bout of bid fever have been fighting their battles with the sort of emotional involvement and ferocity not seen since the late 1960s. Under those conditions fair play rules easily fly out the window.

Junk Bonds

Across the Atlantic the most controversial tactic during Wall Street's own bout of merger mania was the surge in junk bonds. Traditionally junk bonds meant the debt paper issued by companies close to bankruptcy. They might not be totally worthless, like the 'Busted Bonds' of pre-revolutionary Russia or pre-Communist China, but they were highly risky and carried a yield which reflected the fact that they might never be honoured.

During the 1980s, however, junk bonds changed their meaning. A number of investment banks, led by Drexel Burnham Lambert, encouraged clients to issue large numbers of debt securities which could then be used to finance a takeover by means of a shell company. If the bonds were not guaranteed by the parent company of the shell they were junk in themselves. Any value they had came about through the assets of the target they would be used to take over.

In 1981, it was estimated, some $1.4 billion of new junk bonds were issued. By 1985 that total had swollen to $15 billion. In the December the Federal Reserve Board decided that enough was enough. After a brief flurry it changed its rules so that companies could only finance a maximum of half a takeover by means of junk bonds. The minnows which had been eagerly snapping up giants through this tactic were halted in their tracks.

Back in Britain some observers waited for the Takeover Panel to follow suit. It did not. In the first place debt securities had not become quite the rage that they had in the US. Where issued they were usually sold to institutions who, as professionals, could be expected to look out for the risks attached. In any case the Takeover Code already contained clear bans on financing a takeover by means of the target's assets. Finally the British authorities already had broader powers to investigate any takeover which they feared might not be realistically financed.

It was this broad provision which Elders IXL ran into when it decided to try and swallow Allied Lyons, which was three times its own size. Elders' only way to achieve this was through a highly leveraged takeover, financed largely through borrowings. Elders persuaded a consortium of international banks to put up £1.2 billion of the £1.6 billion offer price. Initially Elders planned the financing through a shell company in which the banks would be shareholders. The Takeover Panel disallowed this on the grounds that such a structure might mean that the banks and not Elders were making the takeover. When Elders restructured the arrangement so that the banks were lending it the funds under more normal conditions the Monopolies Commission decided to step in. It was not satisfied that Elders was financially sound at that level of borrowing.

The reaction of the authorities on each side of the Atlantic was different; the problems they were tackling were not the same. The causes, however, were identical: in the grip of takeover fever aggressive companies saw no reason to let size stop them launching an attack. If they had to borrow to the hilt to buy something much larger, then borrow they would. The Monopolies Commission might be able to step in to cases like Elders where the enormous scale of the borrowings had been clearly flagged by attempts to present them as something else. Down the league table smaller companies with lower profiles were gearing themselves up nearly as heavily without attracting much attention.

123

Morgan Crucible

One of the lingering mysteries of the 1985 bid scene was the profit forecast employed by Morgan Crucible in its takeover of First Castle Electronics, a specialist defence electronics company. Morgan Crucible had suffered badly during the recession of the early 1980s, but a combination of new management and the lifting of the general industrial gloom had set it back on the road to recovery. By 1985 it was ready to turn aggressor, undertaking three successive bids in that year, all eventually successful.

Last on the list was First Castle on which Morgan Crucible pounced in December. In the heated takeover climate of the time the bid would not have attracted much attention, at £37 million it was far too small, but for one curious factor. During the early stages of the bid Crucible forecast that 1985 profits would hit £18 million, up from the greatly recovered £15.5 million of 1984. At least that is what its offer document said. Anyone who took the trouble to visit the London offices of Crucible's solicitors, Clifford Turner, would have been given a different picture. Internal documents on show at Clifford Turner contained a profit forecast of £1.3 million lower.

Profit forecasting is a serious matter at any time. During a takeover it can be critical. The Takeover Panel insists on the utmost stringency when forecasts are made. In Crucible's case the internal document was withdrawn, the higher forecast was adhered to, and in the event Crucible actually made £18.7 million in the 1985 year.

It remains unclear, however, just why or how there came to be two different forecasts in existence at the same time. Throughout the bid battle the mystery continued to cast its shadow. Before it was finally able to take over First Castle, Crucible was forced to increase its bid twice; first to £42 million, and then to £48 million. Critics sourly attributed the difficulty Crucible encountered to the profit forecast mystery. Some went so far as to say that Crucible was trying to have its cake and eat it too. It wanted to impress First Castle with its recovery (hence the £18 million) but it wanted a let out if things turned sour at the last moment. The Takeover Panel is very hard on companies which miss their forecasts. This, it was alleged, explained the £16.7 million figure in Clifford Turner's possession.

The accusations were certainly unfounded, representing only how hot tempers become in contested takeovers. Once the Clifford Turner document was withdrawn, the position was clarified. It is true, though, that Crucible's shares languished for part of the bid at a fraction under 200p. Not until it was known that Robert Holmes à Court's Australian company Bell Resources, had built up a stake of 11 per cent did Crucible's shares rise to nearly 250p.

Trusthouse Forte

Takeover tactics do not end when the bid battle draws to a close, just as they should not start only after a bidder has come into view. To be continuously successful as an aggressor, a predatory company must also remember to protect itself from takeover. As already discussed not even the largest or more hyper-active company can feel safe from threat. A few organizations have share structures which act very much in the same way as 'poison pills'. Only a limited number of shares, tightly controlled, carry the real voting power. The bulk of those in issue cannot out vote them. The Savoy Hotel group is probably the most highly publicized example. Ever since the turn of the decade Trusthouse Forte had owned a simple majority of the Savoy's shares, and Lord Forte, the country's most colourful caterer and hotelier, made no secret of his burning ambition to bring the Savoy within his empire.

For six years or more the D'Oyly Carte family and its friends at the Savoy were able to hold Charles Forte at bay by a structure which gave the handful of B shares four times the voting power of the A shares Forte and the public could lay their hands on. This archaic structure, which contravened the basic principle of equal rights for all shareholders, became a cause célèbre in the early 1980s, but the Stock Exchange refused to intervene. Despite intense pressure from the pension funds the Exchange insisted that its only responsibility was to ensure that any unusual voting structure was properly disclosed. It did not choose to force all companies into the same strait-jacket of one share, one vote.

Conclusion

The Stock Exchange's ruling over voting structure was regarded at the time as a rare departure from the Exchange's traditional adherence to the principle of share-holder democracy. Since then there has been at least one other significant swerving by the Exchange which has led some observers to question the depth of the Exchange's commitment to the principle.

In 1985 the Exchange proposed to relax the rule by which any planned new issue of shares had first to be offered to existing shareholders. It was prepared to change its rules to allow even large issues of shares to be placed with selected investors thus undermining the pre-emption rights of existing shareholders.

The pension funds opposed the change on principle. Although they stand to be the main beneficiaries of the change being the largest institutional group they are also shareholders and believe that their rights as shareholders should be protected. So far the Stock Exchange has declined to listen to the pension funds. It claims force majeure. Shareholders' pre-emption rights in the US have already been much eroded by similar measures, so the London Stock Exchange claims that it cannot resist this international precedent.

The arguments over the Savoy's voting structure and shareholders' pre-emption rights are not the only ones which the pension funds have lost with the Stock

Exchange. Too little credit is in fact given them for attempting to uphold basic principles of investment. They have also played a role in preventing Wall Street arbitrageurs from invading British takeover fights except at the fringes. This arises because institutions typically sit out a battle until the bitter end. Although there have been some notable exceptions when the funds have sold out in the market on Day 1, thus giving the predator a priceless base for attack, they are less inclined than private investors to lose their nerve during the contest and sell into the hands of middlemen intent merely on 'passing the parcel' at a profit.

There is one important area, however, where the institutions must be held accountable for fuelling takeover fever, rather than working to improve the returns from British industry. Since the days of the removal of Sir John Davis from Rank Organisation there have been no conspicuous occasions when the pension funds have used their shareholder power to change the executives in their companies.

If the aim of takeovers is to transfer assets into the hands of those who can manage them better, there is at least one other way in which the same aim can be met — by changing managers. Small individual shareholders are rarely in a position to be able to achieve this. The institutions do have the power. They rarely exercise it. Yet at a time when share prices are so high that predators have little leeway to work their new managerial magic, it must be cheaper and more effective to swop old management for new without going through the trauma of a takeover.

Side-stepping takeovers should also be in the long-term interests of the institutional shareholders for two other reasons. In the first place mergers between companies simply shrink the institutions' choice of shares to invest in. Moreover they do so effectively at no net gain to the institutions which regularly hold shares in both bidder and target. The offer price merely moves from one pocket to another where the institutions are concerned.

In the second place the pension funds at least do not depend upon inflated share prices in the market for the substance of their own values. The 1986 Budget, in which the Chancellor decided to claw back the growing surpluses mounting in company pension schemes, established the rule that pension funds are to be valued by reference to their income stream i.e. future dividends from their investments rather than capital values in the market. Thus when capital values outstrip dividend growth the pension funds do not gain according to their own professional benchmark.

Market values do matter to insurance companies and unit trusts, of course. The latter are especially vulnerable to short-term performance pressure generated by the public's perception of market prices. Even these two groups, though, rely more heavily on the performance of their dividend income over the longer term. Yet they make little or no attempt to re-educate the public about this significance.

More importantly, the institutions do not appear to be investigating alternatives to takeovers in the pursuit of dividend growth. The frequency and ease with which American shareholders can topple their top executives is regularly commented on in Britain. It occurs here only infrequently, however. Perhaps this is one American tendency which should be encouraged to cross the Atlantic.

The question of changing management by means short of a takeover could be classed as the unused shareholder tactic. Top executives, on the other hand, do not fail to protect themselves against its possible use. In yet another tactic imported from the US most senior executives provide themselves with so called 'golden parachutes' in case they lose office.

The parachute works like this when a takeover looms. As soon as the top executive believes a raider is on the prowl he persuades the board to re-organize his pay on the basis of a continuous rolling contract for as long a period as he can get out of them. Typically this would be a five-year contract which, being rolling, never shrinks below that length of time. If the takeover materializes and is successful, and if our top executive is then given the push, his fall is cushioned by generous compensation for the loss of his next expected five years' salary.

Occasionally the golden parachute fails to open or is sabotaged by the incoming board. One such case was that of Jack Gill, former managing director of Associated Communications. When Robert Holmes à Court seized control of ACC, Gill believed he had arranged a heavily gilded parachute for himself. He was to hit the ground with a thump. The newcomers simply announced that they did not pay compensation to redundant executives and refused to be bound by the decisions of the previous board.

The tactics that have been studied in this chapter are just some of the newer ones which have been prominent during the takeover boom of the mid-1980s. Some have been by way of variations on earlier versions. The Take-over Panel, for instance, has cracked down heavily on advertising during a takeover in an attempt to outlaw the knocking copy used to such effect in the battles for Distillers and Imperial. This will not prove the end of the matter. In the late 1970s the Panel also felt obliged to restrict advertising following Dalgety's bid for Spillers. It must be a safe bet that a further clamp-down will be needed in another few years or even sooner, if the bright sparks in the merchant banks can find a way round the new restrictions.

Meanwhile the standard array of tactics is steadily increased as principals and advisers seek the advantage of surprise, attempt to undermine their opponent's claim to better management and performance, or try to wrong foot their earnings record or profits forecast. It falls to the Takeover Panel to keep this battery of tactics within some acceptable ethical framework. It is a formidable task at the quietest of times. When bid fever is raging it imposes immense strains on the small team of executives at the Panel, mainly seconded from the merchant banks to which they will return. The recent tendency for victims of the fever to scurry to the courts by way of an appeal against a Panel judgement increases the pressure for the Panel, together with other City authorities, to become less voluntary in its regulation, and move closer to becoming a statutory body. One may deplore the trend; but it seems necessary to beat today's predators at their own game.

9

The City

As always the City's way of doing things was all its own. Takeover fever certainly hit the Square Mile — possibly even more than anywhere else. The reasons however were quite different and so was the outcome. While there were exceptions, as a general rule predators had the upper hand in industrial bids. In the City the reverse was true, with predators much less sure of success when their targets were financial firms.

Since the late 1970s the Stock Exchange had tussled with two apparently intractable problems: the declining share of global securities turnover; and a trading and membership structure which technically infringed the Government's anti-restrictive trading practices legislation. The Exchange had a good defence against the latter; its restrictions were part of maintaining an orderly and decently regulated marketplace. They operated to protect investors not threaten them.

But successive governments turned a deaf ear, largely, it seems, because they feared that releasing the Stock Exchange from the legislation (albeit on logical grounds) would lead the electorate to think Government was favouring the City fat cats.

At about the same time the Council of the Exchange began to believe that part of the reason the London market was losing its international share was the very restrictive

131

structure on which Government frowned. From then on, for diametrically different reasons, the Exchange leaders conspired with Ministers of the Crown to destroy the old jobbing system and the philosophy of fixed brokers' commissions.

The first stage of what has come to be called the 'City Revolution', occurred in 1983 when Stock Exchange chairman, Sir Nicholas Goodison, and the then Trade Secretary, Cecil Parkinson, agreed that the Exchange would not be dragged before the Restrictive Practices Court if it agreed that commissions could be freely negotiated between client and broker. Parkinson had other matters on his mind at the time. He was shortly to be drummed out of his Cabinet post for having promised to marry his secretary, pregnant with his child, but then clung to his existing wife. Goodison, on the other hand, knew that international pressures would probably soon sweep away the British market's insistence that a professional could be either a jobber or a broker but not both. Negotiated commissions would only hasten that day by creating matching domestic pressure inside the market.

When Goodison signed his pact with Parkinson, however, he could not have foreseen the degree of change, upheaval and chaos which was to proceed the 'Big Bang'; the day in October 1986 set aside for the abolition of restrictive practices in the market. The sea-change in securities trading was simultaneously being matched by important alterations in the structure of the banking world and by the first overhaul in 30 years of legislation to protect investors. What was to have been an internal 'Big Bang' in the stockmarket, soon became the symbol of a thorough going revolution across the entire financial services industry.

One of the first and most obvious signs of change was the rush of mergers between stockmarket firms and other forms of financial concerns. The jobbers and brokers were looking for financial muscle, the level of capital backing which would let them take big positions in international securities trading. They feared the might of the foreign securities giants, like Merrill Lynch of the US and Japan's Nomura, which could see them off the field unless the British firms grew big—fast.

On the other side of the coin were the banks, insurance companies, building societies and investment houses which wanted to add a securities trading or distribution arm in pursuit of the fashionable goal of becoming financial services supermarkets.

By the spring of 1986, when the Stock Exchange changed its rules to allow non-members absolute control over member firms, only one first division stockbroker and no jobbers remained independent. The new parents ranged from merchant banks like S. G. Warburg, to general investment houses like Mercantile House. Foreigners ended up in control of far fewer securities houses than had been expected. Moreover, 'friendly' European concerns were twice as common as the much feared Japanese or American ones.

As the pace of change elsewhere in the financial services also accelerated, it was not uncommon for two, say investment houses, to merge and then join forces with a stockbroker. What distinguished all of this frenetic City activity from the takeovers in commerce and industry, was that almost all were amicable. Contested takeovers rarely occurred and were even less frequently successful.

Britannia Arrow

Take, for example, the case of Guinness Peat's contested bid for the unit trust group Britannia Arrow. Its eventual failure became an object lesson in City strengths and weaknesses, reinforcing the intangible belief that 'peoples' businesses are special animals which cannot successfully be taken over without the active consent of the people involved.

At the outset Guinness Peat, a financial conglomerate ranging from commodity broking to merchant banking,

133

was thought to have the advantage over Britannia Arrow despite the latter's growing size in the retail end of investment management. Britannia too owned a merchant bank, Singer & Friedlander, but it was not considered to be in the top league while Guinness Peat's Guinness Mahon was included among the blue bloods. Britannia Arrow's chairman was a wily former Cabinet Minister, Geoffrey Rippon, but Guinness Peat's chairman and chief executive was Alistair Morton, seasoned veteran of City battles and fresh from a victorious engagement with the company's previous chairman, Lord Kissin, whom Morton had beaten in a fight judged bloody even by City standards. Moreover Brittania Arrow appeared to have sold the pass early in the preliminaries when the top executive let it be known that they were prepared to sell — and put a price on it.

Two factors were working in Britannia's favour. Its unit trust management business was riding the crest of the world's bull markets. Profits were flowing straight through. Morton could not, therefore, press home his claim to be a better manager. Possibly more important in the battle, though, was the constant barrage of abuse which Rippon and his team kept up *sotto voce* against Morton. Key figures within Singer & Friedlander let it be known that they would buy out their merchant bank rather than merge it with Guinness Mahon. Rippon said Britannia had considered acquiring Guinness Mahon itself and turned it down as poor quality. Unit trust managers promised to find jobs elsewhere if Morton ended up as head of Britannia.

During the course of the battle fortunes ebbed and flowed. At one point Morton unsettled shareholders by pouring scorn on Britannia's unwillingness to produce a profits forecast early in its trading year. He also had with him certain elements of the press who backed him as a winner after the Kissin affair. But finally, if narrowly, Morton lost, mainly on the grounds that shareholders feared victory would turn to dust in his hands if Britannia's staff exited for friendlier pastures.

Jacob Rothschild

What lends strength to the belief that only friendly mergers work in the City is the difficulty even the most expert have in maintaining them. Jacob Rothschild's experience is a case in point.

Rothschild's story properly begins in 1980 when he and his cousin Evelyn had an unsettling row over the future of N. M. Rothschild, and he lost. Few would argue that Jacob is the cleverer of the two men, but he is a restless, buccaneering dealer, while Evelyn is the placid conservator of the family bank's high standing, traditions and comfortable profits. Like the founder of the Rothschild dynasty, Mayer Amschel Rothschild, Jacob Rothschild is a risk taker who might have doubled the bank's riches or might also have bankrupted it.

After the row with Evelyn, Jacob Rothschild set up on his own with a small investment trust, RIT, as inheritance. Within months he had pulled off what was regarded as a very cheeky coup — the takeover of Great Northern Investment Trust for £97 million. Knowing that he is not a very good manager, Rothschild brought in David Montagu, a City heavyweight, and went off to see what other financial services group he could acquire.

By the end of 1982 Rothschild had brought home stockbrokers Kitcat & Aitken, a splendid asset because with it came senior partner Nils Taube, one of the most innovative intellectuals in the stockmarket.

His next foray was to New York where he acquired 50 per cent of L. F. Rothschild, Unterberg, Towbin, a New York investment bank headed by a Louis F. Rothschild who has no connection with the European aristocrats. Some claimed that Jacob Rothschild bought half of the US firm only to spite cousin Evelyn, who wanted 51 per cent for the bank. But, in fact, while the family feud was still a raging fire in his breast, Jacob had also begun to dream of his own dynasty, founded on a financial services conglomerate.

The following year saw the two biggest items in place: a 25 per cent stake in Hambro Life, the life insurance-linked unit trust group which Mark Weinberg had just bought out of the banking family's portfolio; and the whole of the Charterhouse merchant banking and industrial investment group. The imposing new creation was renamed Allied Rothschild Charterhouse, a £1 billion financial services concern which would blaze the way for the 'City Revolution'.

It lasted less than a year. First to crumble was the link with Weinberg. By mid-December 1984 Weinberg and Rothschild amicably agreed that they could never make a linked-life management team work, and Rothschild sold on his stake to Weinberg's choice, BAT Industries. A month later it was the turn of Charterhouse to disappear — sold to the Royal Bank of Scotland.

As consolation for the ending of his conglomerate dreams, however, Rothschild had £40 million in cash, the profit on the sales, and he was free to go back to what he does best — high-risk mega-deals.

This book has already touched on the role of Jacob Rothschild, the dealer. Suffice it to say here that his first deal of this period was entirely successful. Together with Sir James Goldsmith, Australia's Kerry Packer and Italy's Gianni Agnelli, an urbane and charming bunch of marauders, Rothschild advanced on the American paper, insurance and energy group, St Regis, with a very unwelcome $100 million takeover offer. St Regis paid the 'greenmail'; $50 million to see them off.

In terms of City takeover, however, Rothschild had been right about one thing. He showed other would-be founders of financial dynasties just how difficult it is to cement together the different forms of financial services. Eighteen months after he sold off Charterhouse no other entrepreneur has tried to establish a financial services group spanning both the wholesale and the retail frontiers.

Lloyds

Standard Chartered Bank is the fifth largest banking group in Britain. But it is virtually invisible. With less than three dozen branches in the UK all its considerable expertise has been built up abroad, largely in Africa, Asia (including China), the Middle East and the Pacific rim.

The failure to develop a sizeable base in the world's top industrialized countries, particularly in Europe, has plagued Standard Chartered's top management for years. At the start of the 1980s the problem seemed over: Royal Bank of Scotland, which contains the English banking group, Williams & Glyns, was happy with the idea of a £500 million takeover by Standard Chartered.

Before the corks were out of the champagne bottles however, the Hongkong and Shanghai Banking Group, one of the world's richest banks and the giant in the Hong Kong pool, so well known to Standard, decided to muscle in on this merger. The original deal, being quiet and gentlemanly, might have slipped past the censors. But with the Honkers and Shankers in the ring, the battle suddenly became heated and noisy, forcing the authorities to pay attention.

Eventually both contestants lost out. The Monopolies Commission ruled in January 1982 that Royal Bank should stay Scottish and independent. For the Hongkong and Shanghai Banking Group the reversal was hardly important. For Standard it proved to be the most troublesome failure in its more than a century of existence. Much as it looked it could not find a convincing replacement for Royal Bank; and one became visibly needed as profits went ex-growth for the first time in more than a decade.

Investors shared the board's worries about the failure of the expansion plans almost from the outset. They had some justification. Although it was probably unfair of the market to dub as insipid the 12 per cent increase in 1981 pre-tax profits, the next set of interims revealed that something was wrong: they were down by 28 per cent, the first decline ever.

By this time life was becoming difficult for any international banker. Recession gripped the industrialized world and drove Third World countries into crippling debt. Under its highly experienced chief executive, Peter Graham, Standard in fact rode out the storms relatively well. Having a former Chancellor of the Exchequer, Lord Barber, as chairman, was a further critical asset. There were also some useful strategic acquisitions, notably of MAIBL, the consortium bank previously shared among Midland, the Toronto-Dominion Bank of Canada, Westpac, Australia's largest finance group and Standard itself.

Profits for the whole of 1982 came out just 7 per cent down at £242 million and Standard took the opportunity of a lift in the shares to make a near £100 million rights issue, though at a deep 90p discount to the then market price of around 480p. More light relief was felt after the announcement of the half-time figures for 1983 when Standard's relative immunity from the problems of Latin America was seen as a plus.

There was still plenty for investors to brood over however — South Africa, for instance. Standard has a major presence throughout Africa, from Nigeria to Zimbabwe. But its strongest and historic base is in South Africa, where Standard Bank Investment Corporation (Stanbic), is the second largest after Barclays. Throughout the early 1980s, Stanbic produced excellent profits, notwithstanding a savage economic recession in South Africa. Politically, it was quite otherwise, and Standard opted to reduce its exposure to international abuse by reducing its stake in Stanbic to 42 per cent and South Africa's contribution to group profits from almost one-third to under one-sixth.

In a more respectable part of the world, the USA to be

138

precise, Standard also seemed to have the knack of squeezing profits out of operations which were causing competitors serious problems. Its Union Bank of California, bought in 1979, flourished while local California groups even on the scale of Bankamerica floundered, and Midland Bank's Crocker subsidiary was a full-blown disaster.

Yet the elusive major acquisition continued to escape Standard and earnings per share were battered by heavy provisions against bad debts as the international recession ground on. Around this time Peter Graham retired and the market sourly questioned whether his successor, Michael McWilliam would have the expertise to turn Standard back into a growth stock. It was particularly hard on McWilliam that he stepped into the front line as the bull market became a raging inferno. Mcwilliam is a naturally cautious banker, prepared to nurture profits, like clients, for a long time. From 1984 investors were interested in little more than tomorrow's share price rise.

McWilliams set about building up a merchant banking arm by clever poaching of individuals from other merchant houses, notably Lazards. He charmed his way into the inner circle of 16 foreign banks given operating licences in Australia. He forged close links with building societies such as Bristol & West and Northern Rock, and let it be known that Standard would seek to take over a building society once new legislation allowed the societies to become suitable corporate structures.

However he set his face firmly against the glamour path to the 'City Revolution'. 'We will not be buying a stockbroker or a jobber', he said. 'Few of the planned financial conglomerates will work or last. Let others be the guinea pigs. There will be plenty of opportunities later.' But investors were dazzled by the glamour and high with bid fever. So Standard's shares languished. Neither a strong profits growth in the first half of 1985, nor a well timed $330 million takeover of United Bankcorp of Arizona in September of that year, revived the shares. Midland Bank was forced to sell Crocker. Lloyds also pulled out of California. Standard's Union Bank continued to steam ahead but the shares ignored the fact.

In the spring of 1986 the shares suddenly began to spurt ahead. Was it belated recognition of Standard's fundamental strengths? Not in this market. The rise of more than 130p in the share price in March was fuelled by one thing only — bid rumours. First reports suggested that Royal Bank was planning a suitable revenge on its erstwhile predator by turning raider itself. Then a foreign consortium was mentioned, a logical idea in view of Standard's conspicuous international successes and equally visible domestic weaknesses.

The predator which finally appeared was none other than Lloyds Bank, one of the Big Four High Street names. Under its chairman, Sir Jeremy Morse, Lloyds had held aloof from the scramble to merge with other financial services groups ahead of the 'Big Bang'. Apart from acquiring a string of provincial estate agents Sir Jeremy seemed to prefer that Lloyds should grow its own internal capacities for the 'City Revolution'.

When a particularly juicy opportunity flashed past, however, Sir Jeremy's famous intellectual detachment counted for little. He too, it seems, has an acquisitive streak and must follow it even in the rarefied climate of banking where such upheavals are almost unknown; the last major takeover in High Street banking being the merger between Westminster and National Provincial in the late 1960s. Yet Sir Jeremy retained at least a degree of objectivity. Although Standard's share price had roared up to nearly 880p, Lloyds insisted in the long lead up to its formal offer document that 750p was the price it was sticking to. If Sir Jeremy was gambling on a collapse in Standard's market price, he had a certain stroke of luck. At the beginning of May the market went into reverse and Standard's price slipped downwards.

In traditional fashion Lloyds and Standard Chartered spent a leisurely pre-fight period in verbal battle — something both sides seemed to enjoy to the hilt. Lloyds' one attempt at outlining industrial logic was shot down by Standard. 'Standard is in areas where we are not', said Lloyds' chief executive Brian Pitman. 'With good cause', retorted McWilliam: 'We don't like your areas'. Eventually Lloyds found the battle to acquire a British bank no easier than any of its predecessors. Although it fought to the bitter end, it failed to absorb Standard.

Mercantile

While Lloyds and Standard were squaring up, an earlier attempt at creating an international financial group was fraying at the seams. Back in 1982 John Barkshire, the founding father of the London International Financial Futures Exchange, decided that his own financial services company, Mercantile House, should grow bigger, fast. In a deal which raised eyebrows for its size, audacity and controversial funding, Barkshire paid $90 million for the New York investment house of Oppenheimer. With it he got a mixed bag of retail pooled fund management, wholeseale trading in securities, a valuable futures and bullion trading operation, and a primary dealer in US Government bonds.

Later Mercantile tacked on a British stockbroker, Laing & Cruickshank. Just, however, as it was beginning to look like a well-rounded international group, the Oppenheimer elements began to pull away from the core. Critics of the original deal had claimed that Mercantile would not be able to retain the Oppenheimer partners who had personally shared $60 million in cash in the 1982 takeover. In fact they stayed for more than three years, but the independence of the personally wealthy finally came through. Not all the Oppenheimer operations were lost to Mercantile in the spring of 1986; nor all the creative talent. But the retail fund management business walked away and key personnel began to drift from the wholesale side as well. Suddenly Mercantile was no longer looking like a unified international financial services group but more like the moneybroker it had always been, plus an incomplete collection of other businesses on both sides of the Atlantic.

Conclusion

The sad examples of Jacob Rothschild and John Barkshire brought home to the City just how difficult it is to form and hold together that sort of operation. Both men are undeniably clever and were intensely committed to the strategies they had chosen. Both are motivated, passionate and surefooted in the financial jungle. Neither man has been destroyed by his failure to build a financial conglomerate — Rothschild is happily wheeling and dealing, and Barkshire still has a solid group of profitable businesses to run. But for the time being the City views them both mainly as object lessons in risk taking.

Rothschild seems to have come unstuck when he tried to weld a large retail sales operation (Mark Weinberg's unit linked insurance business then called Hambro Life) onto an equally well-established merchant banking group at Charterhouse. Barkshire hit the rocks of cultural differences between America and Britain. Both were examples of the culture shock which besets financial services.

Cross-border culture shock is the most visible and most frequent. So frequently does it occur that to fear its arrival is regarded in City circles as unimpeachable prudence. It explains why so many senior partners of stockbroking firms spent sleepless nights worrying about the consequences of Merrill Lynch's entry to the London market. The 'Thundering Herd', to give Merrill its Wall Street sobriquet, could snap up any of the UK players for little more than petty cash, after all. As it happens Merrill has been conspicuous by its absence from the lists of marauders. It too fears the problems of yoking together the British and American ways of doing business.

There is nothing inevitable about the future of financial

conglomerates, on the other hand. They are not doomed to failure. At present most of the fears are just that; the 'City Revolution', ushered in by October's 'Big Bang' has hardly begun. It is far too early to judge its consequences. By the same token the infant conglomerates now being formed are as yet untried. Claims for their ability to resist culture shock are made in hope not out of experience.

One or two look distinctly promising, however, and ironically in face of the wide-felt fears that international giants would make all the running, the top two contenders are all-British. One of the two has been formed by Barclays Bank out of an alliance with stockbrokers, de Zoete and Bevan, and jobbers, Wedd Durlacher, the largest firm in the jobbing fraternity. BZW, as it is already known, is designed to be a major force in securities trading. Its main competitor, dubbed the 'Swarm' in conscious parody of Merrill Lynch's nickname, is an even more ambitious merger. It brings together merchant bankers, S. G. Warburg, blue blooded jobbers, Akroyd & Smith, and two stockbrokers — Rowe & Pitman, which probably has the greatest placing power in the London market, and gilts specialists, Mullens, home of the Government Broker until the abolition of that function during the 'City Revolution'. In a number of permutations these four will combine under Warburg's parentage to form the Mercury International Group, a more asset-management-oriented business than BZW.

Two of the City's most imposing merchant banking figures head up the two giants: Warburg's David Scholey at Mercury, and Sir Martin Jacomb who came to BZW from Kleinwort Benson via a stint as deputy chairman of the Council for the Securities Industry, a Bank of England regulatory failure which Jacomb helped to bury. The differences in the designs of their new operations mirror their personal characters. Scholey is the deal-maker, at home in the hurley-burley of bitter takeover battles and a great salesman of Warburg's investment management skills to insurance companies and pension funds. Jacomb is more the pure banker, understanding the risks and rewards of taking positions as a principal in the financial marketplace. It is not just the individuals though who supply the differences. Both BZW and Mercury betray their origins; the one in Britain's largest clearing bank, the other in its most entrepreneurial merchant bank. It may be cruel of the City to see the forthcoming struggle between them as one between deep pockets and talent, but Barclays certainly has the funds and Warburg the fleetness of foot.

What BZW and Mercury have in common with nearly all the other aspiring City conglomerates is that they arise from amicable mergers. Contested takeovers in the City are more rare than elsewhere and for good reason. It is well-nigh impossible to shackle individuals to a particular employer, however heavily gilded the golden handcuffs. And above all, City firms are people businesses. An exodus of even a handful of key staff can destroy a financial services firm. Their willingness to merge is a *sine qua non* of success in financial takeovers. What is most surprising about this bout of bid fever is that so many predators have forgotten this fundamental fact in the euphoria of hyper-activity.

10

Prospects and Warnings

Throughout the boom in takeovers, right into the summer of 1986, there were those who continued to argue that they were a healthy phenomenon; that British industry was awakening from torpor; that new and effective managements were sweeping the dust from sleepy boardrooms.

Their numbers dwindled, however, as the months passed. By the beginning of the summer of 1986 merger supporters were well outnumbered by those who publicly expressed dismay about the level of takeover activity. One of the most influential of these was Sir Gordon Borrie. As Director General of the Office of Fair Trading (OFT) he studied as a matter of course all bids for assets totalling more than £30 million. He was also responsible for executing the Government's Competition Policy, and it was usually on his recommendation that a bid would be referred to the Monopolies Commission. The formal power was necessarily vested in the Trade Secretary who could, and occasionally did, run counter to Sir Gordon's advice. But any Secretary of State contemplating such a course knew that he risked controversy — or worse. Thus when Sir Gordon's annual report for 1985 expressed serious misgivings about the current merger mania, most industrial and financial leaders took note.

Sir Gordon Borrie

In early June 1986 Sir Gordon was just about to enter his third five-year term of office. His pronouncements, therefore, carried the weight of ten years of experience in dealing with takeovers of every kind. This was what he had to say:

'Concern has been expressed — with which I have sympathy — as to whether the frothy and almost hysterical merger boom which was building up at the end of 1985 was an entirely healthy phenomenon. The substantial costs of mounting and defending bids must all be met ultimately from the profits of the businesses which are bought and sold. These transactions make heavy demands on management time and it has been suggested that the constant threat of takeover may have an undesirable effect on companies' strategic planning.'

Sir Gordon could not be accused of blind prejudice. Apart from all the experience which preceded his words of caution, he also revealed himself to be favourably inclined towards takeovers in the normal course of events. Then, he averred, they were 'part of the competitive process and I should be the last to argue for extra protection for sleepy and inefficient managements'. Nor was he intimidated by size. Noting that during 1985 the term 'mega-bid slipped into the parlance of financial, economic and political commentators', for his part it was 'almost irrelevant' that the 'assets of a target company amounted to more than a billion pounds'. Sir Gordon kept firmly in mind that he was there to protect the public interest and to stop mergers which might act against it. He concluded that: 'bigness may or may not be beautiful but under my scrutiny it is certainly not automatically bad'.

Although couched in the temperate language of the professional Civil Servant, Sir Gordon's message was clear enough. He took it for granted that his audience would

146

concur that boom conditions existed in takeovers. He was nearly as sure that they would accept that much of the activity was 'frothy and almost hysterical'. From that firm base he felt able to allege that an atmosphere of bid fever cost management time and money, and interfered with their central obligation, to devise a company's strategy.

By the time Sir Gordon came to make his warning his status as 'honest broker' between Government and commerce was fully recovered from the bruises it had received during battles with certain Trade Secretaries earlier in the decade. Particularly during the ministry of Lord Cockburn, but also when Cecil Parkinson was Trade Secretary, the advice of the OFT had been rejected, on occasion with humiliating publicness. Sir Gordon was still flying the flag of Competition Policy from his own safe seat in the OFT while both Lord Cockburn and Parkinson, if for different reasons, had almost vanished from Government function.

Regulation

In his annual statement Sir Gordon Borrie referred not only to the unprecedented size of the bids being carried through, he also described their conduct in the same vein. So concerned was he about the latter that he felt obliged to make two specific points relating to bid tactics. He confirmed what everyone had long suspected that Elders IXL's bid for Allied Breweries had been referred to the Monopolies Commission because it: 'demonstrated in an extreme form the new trend to mount bids with borrowed money'. Elders, it will be recalled, arranged a consortium of international banks to provide £1.25 billion of the £1.8 billion offer price.

Sir Gordon also thought it necessary to comment on the upsurge in advertising during takeovers. He wrily asked whether companies thought such advertising gave value for money. He was unimpressed by most ad campaigns and thought that shareholders would be likewise.

Sir Gordon's philosophical remarks however were also important for what they revealed about the relationship between the Government and the City in regulating bids. Sir Gordon can concentrate on competition and the public interest while choosing to note a new trend in bid tactics, precisely because the Government can rely on the City, in the shape of the Takeover Panel in the main, to look after the conduct of takeovers.

That relationship is fundamentally unaltered by the new Financial Services legislation and the semi-statutory position of the Securities and Investments Board. It is also true that at no time does the regulation of the City keep it totally free of sharp practice let alone downright knavery. Just as Sir Gordon's department feels confident to deal with an era of mega-bids, when total takeover activity in terms of assets has more than doubled each year from 1984, so the main City authorities also look to be robust enough to withstand plenty of shocks.

What is much less certain is the unshakeability of Government Competition Policy. Sir Gordon may be clear that he is charged with investigating matters of public good. A succession of Secretaries of State have made it equally clear that they are just as concerned with matters of pure size. Or are they? Company chairmen regularly complain about the lack of clear guidelines from Government about acquisitions. On occasion it has seemed unmistakable that Government seeks to prevent the formation of a monopoly in any market even if it is benign. Companies believe that Government will seek to prevent them annexing more than 25 per cent of an identifiable market.

On other occasions, however, companies with manifestly more than 25 per cent have been allowed to grow even more dominant by acquisition even though their case, to commercial eyes, may appear mere window dressing and sophistry.

In November 1985 the Government promised a review of its Competition Policy. Six months later it began the process of structuring the review which was promised for early winter. Industry's hopes were not high; previous reviews which had satisfied politicians had barely addressed the issues on which companies sought guidance: namely, fixed and obvious conditions by which all take-overs would be judged. Sir Gordon Borrie's annual statement had not kindled commerce's hopes. He was profoundly content with the pragmatic approach to mergers by which each was separately considered. Companies wanted to know in advance whether one course or another would be open to them. They wanted clarity not pragmatism or 'uncertainty' as they redubbed Borrie's approach.

In any case early hints suggested that the Competition Policy review might be more productive in the administrative area than in the philosophical. The review committee was charged with seeing whether references could be speeded up. They were also to try and devise a way of referring a bid to a Monopolies Commission inquiry without it being branded unacceptable in advance of the evidence.

These issues were admittedly important — company chairmen frequently grumbled at the sluggishness of the monopolies commission inquiries and at the way the mere fact of having been referred was interpreted as *prima facie* evidence that a bid was outside the public interest. At the same time they represented minor concerns compared with the great questions of which bids would be permitted and which would not.

Guinness had been permitted to bid for Distillers (even though it already owned Bells and would become at a stroke the world's largest Scotch distiller) after agreeing to dispose of a limited number of minor brands. United Biscuits and Imperial were given permission to swop sides after selling Golden Wonder, the dominant brand of potato crisps. Sir Gordon Borrie considered that these cases actually clarified the Government's policy on large-scale bids. British companies were not so sure.

They were happier with the basic framework of rules

149

which governed the takeovers themselves. Despite regular carping British business had considerable confidence in the workings of the Takeover Panel, although, as already shown, its voluntary powers were coming under strain from the encroachments of the Statute Book and the Courts onto its patch. It was also facing much greater difficulties in imposing its discipline as the merchant banks, its traditional subjects, escaped into the deregulated and elusive financial conglomerates now forming.

A time bomb was audibly ticking away. In the face of the powerful changes arising out of the 'City Revolution' regulation of corporate affairs, including takeovers, would have to be restructured or the existing mechanics would explode under the strain. But that was for the future. As the details of the Competition Policy review were announced in June 1986 companies were indulging in a traditional pastime, grumbling about the Takeover Panel's draconian limitations on takeover advertising, and wondering whether the Stock Exchange should uphold the pre-emption rights of shareholders in new issues of equity or allow companies to sell shares to friendly outsiders by way of vendor placings.

As T. S. Eliot so sagely observed, the world is much more likely to end with a whimper than a gigantic bang in which everything is consumed. Anyone who witnessed the great stock market crash of 1974 when the index hit 146 knew that he or she was listening to the echoes of the oil price explosion of that year.

The takeover boom of 1984–6 seems more likely to obey Eliot's law. It seems set to peter rather than be snuffed out. Unlike the previous boom in 1972–3 this bout of bid fever was apparently causing no undue strains on the banking fraternity. No secondary banking crisis threatened as it had done in the property lending excesses of that earlier time.

Takeover rules and discipline (though under strain from new and deplorable tactics and the deregulation of financial advisers) was firmly established in 1986. Major changes in the regulatory structures would be needed to cope with the 'City Revolution', but the foundations were strong and robust. In 1968, the last time takeover fever had swept Britain as virulently, the Takeover Panel had not even been thought of. Its foundations, in fact, arose out of the excesses of that time.

Nevertheless, warning signals did flash occasionally from the regulatory authorities. Sir Gordon Borrie might reflect with pleasure that the Office of Fair Trading was able to cope with the £15 billion of mergers with which it was confronted in 1985, compared with only £6 billion in 1984. His annual statement barely concealed his fears about the effect of a sustained period of such hyper-activity. The future role of the Takeover Panel was the subject of somewhat anxious study by the Bank of England, the Securities and Investments Board and the Stock Exchange.

These regulatory signals, however, were less urgent than those beginning to emerge from the commercial sector itself. More than half of all takeovers eventually disappoint their sponsors. It has been shown already how many of the great predators of the 1968 bout became casualties in the following decade or so. By mid-1986 some of the most aggressive raiders of this latest bout of merger mania were beginning to show possibly fatal flaws.

Hanson Trust

In early June Hanson Trust, that most acquisitive of all British companies, announced pre-tax profits for the six months to 31 March up by 49 per cent to £157.6 million, and that with no contribution from Imperial Group which was not formally engulfed until just after the end of that period.

Stockmarket reaction to this extraordinary burst of profits was to mark the shares down by 2p to 183p. The influential Lex column of the *Financial Times* sourly noted that Hanson gave away little, if any, information about

151

the results but it seemed that the gains had not come through the operating profits of the businesses so frequently acquired. South Africa's bitter problems, which had once again hit the Rand, had wiped out the trading profits of Ever Ready Batteries. London Brick, trying to rebuild market share by holding down prices, was a mystery. In the US, said Lex, the latest acquisition, SCM, was driving along with its titanium dioxide business doing well, and the core typewriter operations back in profit. The older US acquisitions were making progress at a rate of less than 10 per cent in dollar terms.

Hanson's growth was coming from financial management of its cash pile in Britain and its dollar loans, and deals. Lord Hanson had always been adept at property dealing, for instance, and he did not appear to have lost his touch when it came to the carve-up of the Allders store group, all that remained of UDS which Hanson had bought to break up in 1982.

Earnings per share were also up by 25 per cent at the interim stage, so the Hanson touch was clearly good for shareholders, especially as dividend policy was generous. The market however was starting to question the quality of earnings and even to ask itself whether Hanson Trust was the right long-term environment for businesses to grow in.

Storehouse

If Lord Hanson's experience showed that a company which can only grow by way of deals soon meets a jaded market, Sir Terence Conran revealed another classic flaw in over-ambitious takeover: they frequently do not perform as promised in the glossy offer documents.

About the same time as Hanson was unveiling the phenomenal interim profits which the market treated so cavalierly, Sir Terence had a pretty sorry picture to paint at the Storehouse Group, newly formed from the merger of his Habitat–Mothercare conglomerate with British Home Stores.

That merger had cost Sir Terence the friendship of Ralph Halpern, the Burton chief, and the chance to take up 20 per cent of Debenhams, Halpern's latest acquisition. Now Storehouse was failing to live up to the projections made so confidently only a few months before. BHS was to pull out of food retailing with the loss of 2000 jobs. No hint of the problems of competition among the supermarket chains had surfaced in the takeover documents. 'Now', the new fashion chain aimed at teenagers and women in their early twenties, was also to close. It had been a 'mistake' Conran candidly admitted, too closely associated with Mothercare in the eyes of shoppers.

Back in February, when Conran had put the merger together, it had seemed one of the more logical in the retail sector. In June, when Sir Terence announced the BHS food withdrawal and the closure of 'Now' the market was inclined to reward him for tackling the problems so swiftly. On the day Storehouse's shares even rose by 10p to 300p. This still left them 60p below their buoyant launch value, and trailing the rest of the retail sector by 20 per cent.

Conran still had his supporters, however. They simply dug themselves in as they learned that it would take longer for the Conran magic to lift BHS than it had done for him to turn round Mothercare. Still, they were confident that it could be done and indeed the financial results did show some glowing corners. A more profound worry was generated by the fear that even Conran would find it difficult to repeat the Mothercare trick. There he had revitalized a tired formula. How many more times could that be done? The High Street is a cruel place for those who cannot keep it supplied with fresh concepts.

Argyll

In Scotland, Argyll Group's James Gulliver was brooding over another feature of acquisitiveness: a predator cannot afford to lose. Admittedly the whole market was in difficulties, as institutional appetites were bloated with calls on their cash, but that was not not the main reason that Argyll's shares had fallen to 325p, their low for the year.

Put simply, investors were beginning to think that Gulliver might have lost his touch. Back at the end of 1985, when Gulliver opened the battle for Distillers, Argyll's shares appeared to move up each week in defiance of the rule that defender moves up, bidder drops away to reflect the cost of acquisition.

Then along came Guinness, thought to be safely tucked away with Bells, and spoiled Gulliver's dream. In a bid battle stuffed with dirty tricks, advertising slanging matches, appeals to the courts, and all the ramshackle baggage of modern bid bitterness Guinness's Ernest Saunders out-manoeuvred Gulliver. The market's unsympathetic conclusion was that Argyll had aimed too high and, like Icarus, was due for a fall.

Markets are organic entities. There is no standing still in them as Distillers had learned to its cost. So, as Argyll was judged unsuccessful as a predator so it came to be thought of as itself vulnerable to takeover. Investors, like any other mob, enjoy the spectacle of predator turned prey; barely had the idea been voiced than it began to gain credence in the marketplace. Some commentators remarked that only the chance of a bid sustained Argyll's shares at around 75 per cent of its high for the year.

Foster

Nor were the liabilities all concentrated at the mega end of the takeover bustle. Smaller companies too, found themselves with a sour aftertaste after indulging their acquisitive streak. One such was John Foster, the spinner and cloth maker. In May 1986 Foster's profits for the year to the end of February were discovered to be £1.13 million, only a small way ahead of the £1.1 million of the previous year.

Acquisitions were blamed, particularly fashion group, Pepper Lee, Foster's most recent attempt at modest diversification. The targets had brought greater headaches than anyone at Foster had expected. They had also cost more in good hard cash. That was not all. In pure trading terms, before allowing for the burdens of the acquisition campaign, Foster was lagging dismally behind its historic peak, back in the mid-1970s.

Foster was not alone in having failed to regain past peaks even through a determined acquisition strategy. Many other industrial groups were still looking wistfully back to 1979: enough to make a nonsense of claims that current astronomical bid prices were justified by the quantum leap in prospects for British companies.

A multitude of other companies could also confirm Foster's sour experience with acquisitions undertaken with such high hopes. Sir Gordon Borrie was echoing a long string of commentators when he observed that an acquisitive streak makes heavy demands on management time and energy. He argued that the constant threat of takeover distracted a defending board from its long-term strategy planning. He might have argued that it also deflects the predator from the slow, careful nurturing of existing businesses.

Cover Up

Natural predators, unlike Foster, do not easily confess to the failure of their acquisition campaign. Their characters inhibit them from confessing to failure of any kind. But that is only part of the cause; they also hide failures from themselves by a multitude of disguises.

The commonest manoeuvre is the 'never stand still long

enough to be caught ploy'. If you take over a succession of companies swiftly enough the latest acquisition will disguise the tailing off in its predecessors. In turn that will need to seek the shadows of a following purchase. So this manoeuvre shackles the predator to an unending chain of takeovers. Should suitable targets run short in one business sector, there is nothing for it but to switch to a new sector. This route leads to a mixed collection of businesses and the day, possibly not too far into the future, when investors will wake up to the lack of coherence and logic.

'Break up' is a variation of the 'never stand still' manoeuvre. Once known as 'asset stripping' these days it is motivated less from greed than need. If, having bought a collection of companies, it is possible to sell off chunks at a good price, do so at once. Critics will probably be unable to follow through the complex paper work, and even if the rump proves to perform less than brilliantly it can always be claimed that it effectively cost nothing.

True asset stripping is a pre-determined plan, based on an assessment that the parts are worth more than the whole. Break-ups more frequently occur as a reaction to the bleak realities which stand revealed on completion day. It is true that the target company's best assets are stripped out in a break-up but this is not normally planned in advance.

Some professional raiders, such as Lord Hanson, do have a break-up philosophy which is more akin to asset stripping. With them, it is pre-arranged that the target will be split up. The game plan is to achieve this with the maximum profit in the shortest time. Both United Dominions Stores (UDS) and the American SCM (the old Smith Corona typewriters group) fell into Hanson's clutches when he intended to break them up. So advanced is his philosophy, that it is never possible to tell when the break ups have finished, and the job of growing the rump has begun.

By 1983 the main sales of parts of UDS seemed complete. Hanson had chosen to keep the Allders chain of second rank department stores. In 1986 some of those also came under the hammer. Within weeks of the mighty takeover of SCM a similar programme of disposals netted $250 million and retained the core typewriter businesses together with some typically Hanson-type basic but high earning operations, like the titanium dioxide division. Whether that would be the final shape of SCM in Hanson's hands was anyone's guess. But by now it was already impossible to untangle the multitude of transactions and tease out a true picture of earnings and return on investment.

The 'foie gras' tactic is the reverse of the 'break-up' but can be used to the same effect. Instead of breaking up and selling on parts of the acquisition until it is impossible to guess the original cost of the remaining sections, the idea is to keep stuffing the original purchase with new bits and pieces until a similar confusion prevails. While the best method requires that the new add-ons are themselves new acquisitions broken off from their parent groups and stuffed into the company to be massaged, it is possible to achieve this by using existing divisions in the acquisitive company. In these cases it usually pays to rename or re-organize divisions so that determined analysts are baulked when they try to look back and compare like with like.

Continuous acquisitions, break-ups or 'stuff 'em' jobs involve hectic activity. Most predators, even the totally committed, finally tire of this ceaseless round of hyper-activity. At this stage investors may well begin to see under the disguise; but with any luck that could be some time in the future and an intervening industrial slump may plausibly be used to explain away poor performance as a hiccup caused by 'adverse international factors outside our control'.

In the meantime there are one or two ways tiring raiders can buy a respite. A favourite cover up of accountancy-trained predators involves presentation of the perform-ance. Most traditional is to consolidate the new division immediately. It thus disappears from sight; and in any moderately sized group becomes impossible to differentiate within the group as a whole.

Merger accounting, a new number-crunching game, has the opposite effect. Its purpose is to single out the new acquisition in the first year after incorporation. Needless to say it is presented in the most flattering light. Merger accounting has caught on because of its beautifying properties. The acquiring company is permitted to load all redundancy, rationalization and re-organization costs on the new company right at the beginning. It can also write off all goodwill in the first year. At the end of that period the purchase can rise like a new born babe, unburdened by past commitments.

Of course the process cannot be repeated the following year so earnings growth could begin to look distinctly unbecoming. It is time for stage 2 to begin. The predator now has a choice: either opt for full consolidation in the hope of swallowing the division within the whole; or buy another company on the 'never stand still' principle. There the hope is that attention will be distracted to the newest deal and yesterday's purchase can be passed off as 'that old thing' as if it had lain in the wardrobe for years.

Precedents

Natural predators do not stand and reflect upon their historical antecedents nor upon the collapse of past bouts of merger mania. If they do pay them brief passing attention it is to spare a moment's sympathy for life's losers. Such animals rarely learn lessons from history. They believe themselves unique or a new breed. They cannot conceive of failure.

Their backers, shareholders and potential investors, on the other hand, can and sometimes do, take time to consider the precedents of history. When they do the conditions which nourish an acquisitive streak can wither like the tundra with the first autumn frost — and just as thoroughly.

158

That process appeared to start in the early spring of 1986. Old timers in the market could be found in corners muttering about the fate which befell so many of the aggressive young bidders of the late 1960s and early 1970s. What happened, they mused, to the promise that merging Thorn with EMI held out? What became of Rolls Royce, stock market darling of the late 1960s? At that time Courtaulds was still aggressively carving out a highway in man-made fibres. Would the recovery of the mid-1980s cancel out all the mighty setbacks and false dawns in between?

Such voices were drowned out by the noise of all those who stood to make a parasitical living off the predators, including a fair sprinkling of institutional fund managers who let short-term performance, which benefits only themselves as individuals, outweigh the long-term returns which benefit the funds they manage.

By the time spring had fully arrived, in late April or thereabouts, different considerations were letting the voices of doubt be heard again. A blockbusting rights issue of more than £700 million from National Westminster Bank, conspicuously lacking in specific reasons, stopped the bull market in its tracks. From then on into the early summer the index drifted aimlessly, recovering one day, shooting down the next.

It was far too early to pronounce the end of the bull trend. Not only Natwest's rights issue but a large number of new issues were calling upon fund managers' cash at a time of year when their pockets are less well lined than usual. The great privatization of British Gas and, possibly British Airways, loomed ahead for the autumn. It was more than likely that the institutions had merely paused for breath. What aroused suspicions was the clamour with which supporters of the bull market insisted that it was only a breathing space. A bad case of protesting too much.

Meanwhile the predators were behaving true to form. Any momentary downturn in the market brought them out in full cry. After all, their targets represented even better value as their market values slipped a little. Dixons, the electricals group intent on becoming queen of the High Street, redoubled its efforts to snap up Woolworth. Lloyds spared no energy in its long-term pursuit of Standard Chartered though the other bank's shares stayed stubbornly above 800p compared with Lloyds' offer of 750p. Dee Corporation pursued a place among the top three supermarket chains by agreeing to buy Fine Fare from Associated British Foods for between £600 and £690 million, depending on how the figures were calculated.

Among the smaller fry, bid activity was most feverish in the engineering sector, possibly because it had been the last to pull out of the recession of the early 1980s. In the electronics industry all attention was focused on the tussle between GEC and Plessey. Although the bid technically had not existed since GEC was referred to the Monopolies Commission in January, the consensus of City opinion was that it was only temporarily suspended. No Government, it was argued, would wantonly stop GEC's strategy for the electronics industry even if that involved it swallowing its leading competitor in telecommunications and defence electronics supplies.

Conclusion

In its later stages the mid-1980s bout of bid fever continued to be characterized by distasteful tactics. Even GEC sued Plessey for libel in the US courts; a counter to Plessey's plea (rejected) to the same courts to have GEC's bid ruled out of court under US law. The Takeover Panel put the lid on advertisements which slanged the opposite side — though history suggested that predators, merchant bankers and advertising agents would sooner or later find a way round the ban. The Bank of England attempted to sit on banks which spent their own money excessively in share raids during clients' bid battles. But the first bank at which the Old Lady pointed a finger, Morgan Grenfell, was able to argue that the restriction should begin after

160

its own deals had been concluded. It was difficult to believe that other merchant banks would not find loopholes to suit their own purposes.

The Stock Exchange's agonising over vendor placings and the pre-emptive rights of existing shareholders was not really central to the takeover issue. Dee Corporation, which spearheaded the use of large-scale vendor placings was still using the attractions of its own paper in a perfectly traditional way in order to mount bids.

This was no case of a minnow trying to turn pike of the pond. Dee was already a young pike when it embarked on the acquisition trail in the mid-1980s. Its move for Fine Fare had considerable logic behind it. Concentration in the supermarket sector was squeezing out all but the totally committed. British Homes Stores and Asda were both ready to concede that only specialists could prosper in the industry. Those who attempted to combine both food manufacturing and food retailing would only fall between two stools, their actions argued.

The only way Dee could break out of the also rans division into the top league was by acquisition. Fine Fare offered both size and the right geographical infill. It was probably also for sale. Dee's chairman, Alec Monk, incubated the Fine Fare deal for two years. It came to term when the market had just slipped from its 1985–6 peak though Dee arguably paid a little too dear. Still the package included a 15 per cent stake in Dee which ABF was happy enough to pick up, and Monk deserved to see his careful strategy succeed.

Earlier Sir Owen Green of BTR had deserved to win both Tilling and Dunlop, even if it was a matter of regret that the institutional shareholders of Tilling were so supine. He deserved them not because, like Alec Monk, he had carefully pinpointed the two objects. BTR had made it clear for years that it was a selective magpie in the industrial sector. In Tilling's case its management needed an injection of fresh blood. An aggressive predator in its day it had begun to rest on its laurels. Tilling's

161

shareholders declined to exert their rights, fire the management, and install new. It was right, therefore, that livelier management seized it by force.

As for Dunlop it had lost its way completely. Homeless, without purpose and shorn of its major products its only hope of existence lay within a multi-purpose industrial group where it could hope to learn new skills or revive old ways from scratch.

BAT's takeover of Eagle Star insurance group, by outbidding the German Allianz insurance industry giant, inspired no such confidence. Neither did the way it was left with Allied Dunbar, the unit trust operation when Jacob Rothschild's grandiose financial supermarket collapsed. BAT might argue that it had planned to make financial services the fourth leg of its enterprise. From the outside the first bid looked like patriotism overcoming commercial commonsense; the second like an unsolicited gift.

Too many of the bids made at that time could not be justified in commercial terms. They were made neither as part of a proper acquisition strategy nor after careful analysis. A few hours reflection seemed to suffice as the basis for buying and selling large chunks of British industry at prices which could not be supported by much more than the hope that future earnings would dramatically outstrip the past.

They were made in the face of evidence that acquisitions are a doubtful road to growth; that they more frequently fail to live up to expectations or claims made at the time. They were made even as recent acquisitions collapsed, crumbled, or simply returned to the uninspired earnings performance they had shown under the pre-acquisition management.

In short, too many were made solely because their authors had an acquisitive streak which they were bent on indulging. Signs of economic revival plus a roaring bull market provided the ideal conditions. Predators are glamorous. Their characters are attractive, their energy

162

draws lesser mortals like a magnet. Where they intervened to raid companies in thrall to ageing managements they were rightly applauded. Both they and their supporters, however, soon lost the knack of identifying the truly moribund. For a time the market too lost its ability to distinguish companies in need of shake up and those which would never set the Thames on fire.

Labour politicians stormed about insanity in the City and threatened to introduce laws which would forbid all mergers which could not prove they were in the public good. All acquisitions in the defence industry would be automatically referred to the Monopolies Commission. All this was hardly sensible but it was an understandable reaction.

There was no avoiding the fact that takeover activity had reached levels which defied logic. The only way of describing this period was in medical terms. Bid fever reached epidemic proportions, invading even the normally immune banking community and stoked by the self-interest of professional advisers of all kinds who earned large fees from their clients' acquisitive habits. So long as the bull market held up, the worst excesses of over-geared bids were avoided, and other calls on institutional cash remained moderate there was little to stop the acquisition minded until their own common-sense returned or the rosy forecasts for industrial growth were replaced by more usual predictions of changeable weather with a tendency to showers.

Index

accounting, 34, 97–8, 157–8
advertising, 43, 54, 57, 58, 83,
    98–100, 109, 121, 129, 147,
    150, 154, 160
Agnelli, Gianni, 136
Akroyd & Smithers, 96, 97, 143
Allders, 10, 54, 152, 156
Allianz, 23–4, 27, 162
Allied Breweries, 10, 74, 110, 115,
    147
Allied Dunbar, 25, 36, 162
Allied Lyons, 39, 74–7, 94, 115, 123
Allied Rothschild Charterhouse, 136
American Thread, 67
arbitrageurs, 11, 25–32, 56, 116, 127
    see also individual headings
Argos, 24
Argyll, 39, 59–61, 66, 85, 118, 119,
    154
asset-stripping, 10, 54, 112, 156–7
Associated British Foods, 38–9, 160,
    161
Associated Communications
    Corporation, 28, 70, 129

B & Q, 72
Bank of England, 1, 58, 81–2, 86, 87,
    120, 143, 151, 160
banks, 1, 17–18, 44, 76–7, 94, 123,
    132, 133, 137–41, 147, 150
    merchant, 16, 21, 34, 80–7, 90–2,
    94, 119–22, 132, 150
    see also individual headings

Barber, Lord, 138
Barclays, 143
Barkshire, John, 141, 142
Bass, 45
BAT Industries, 9, 23–7 *passim*, 33,
    35–7, 136, 162
    BATUS, 9
Bath & Portland, 37
Beazer, C. G., 12, 37
Beckett, John, 72, 73
Beecham, 108
Bell Resources, 125
Bells, 60, 64, 65, 120, 149, 154
Benford Concrete, 12
Berisford, S & W, 11, 72
BICC, 113
Binns Cornwell, 110
Black, Conrad, 6
Blank, Victor, 72
Blyth, Sir James, 42–3
Boesky, Ivan, 27–8, 56
Bond, Alan, 30, 76, 114
Booker McConnell, 38, 75
Borrie, Sir Gordon, 18, 145–9, 151,
    155
Bowater, 55, 56
break-ups, 10, 54, 77, 93, 112, 152,
    156–7
    see also asset-stripping
Brickhouse Dudley, 12
Bristow, James, 47
Britannia Arrow, 133–5
British Airways, 159

British Gas, 159
British Home Stores, 51, 153, 161
British Printing and Publishing
    Corporation, 3, 4
British Sugar, 11–12, 72
British Telecom, 40, 41, 101, 102
brokers, 17, 34, 95–7, 132–3
Brooke Bond, 37
BTR, 19–22, 26, 33, 35, 58–9, 104,
    111, 161
building societies 133, 139
Burton Group, 9, 29–30, 48–52
BZW, 143, 144

Cannon Group, 30, 114
Castlemaine, 30, 75, 76
Cazenove, 95–7
Charter Consolidated, 55, 97
Charterhouse, 136, 142
    Japhet, 72, 73
Chubb & Son, 37
Citicorp, 76
'City Revolution', 81, 87, 95, 132,
    136, 139, 140, 143, 150, 151
Clark, Sir John, 42–4
Clifford Turner, 92, 124, 125
Coats Paton, 55, 56
Cockburn, Lord, 147
Colliers, 52
Comet, 72
commission, 102, 105, 132
competition policy, 5, 41, 54–5, 77,
    91, 92, 94, 146–51
'concert parties', 37, 89, 95
Connell, David, 121
Connell, John, 64–7
Connelly, Philip, 43
Conran, Sir Terence, 48, 51–2,
    152–3
Courtaulds, 44, 55, 159
Crocker Bank, 139, 140
Currys, 71, 84, 107

Dalgety, 99, 120, 121, 129
Davis, Sir John, 21, 110, 127
Debenhams, 29, 31, 48, 50–2, 153
Dee Corporation, 9, 37–9, 160, 161
defence industry, 41, 43, 163
'dirty tricks', 42, 56, 61, 121–2, 154
disclosure, 95

Distillers, 10, 26, 39, 57, 60–1,
    64–8, 82–5, 109, 114–16,
    118–21 passim 129, 149, 154
Dixons, 16–17, 45, 71, 84–5,
    104–5, 107, 160
Drexal Burnham Lambert, 122
drinks sector, 10, 60–1, 64–7, 74–7,
    83–4, 114–16, 120–1, 129,
    154
Dunlop, 58, 161–2
Durham, Sir Kenneth, 73

Eagle Star, 22–7 passim, 33, 35, 162
EEC, 92
Elders, 10, 39, 74, 76–7, 94, 115,
    123, 147
electronics, 40–4, 124–5, 160
Elliott, John, 74, 76, 94
engineering, 12–13, 55, 78, 108, 160
English Sewing Cottons, 45
Entrad, 32, 67–8
Europe, 7, 92, 133
Ever Ready, 57, 152
Evered, 78
Express Newspapers, 3–5 passim,
    69–71

Federal Reserve Board, 122
fees, 85–6, 98, 163
Ferruzzi, 11
Financial Services Act/Bill, 16, 88, 98,
    119, 148
Financial Times Index, 1, 13, 14, 36,
    77, 108, 150, 159
Financial Weekly, 4
financing, bid, 13, 24, 38, 39, 76–7,
    87, 94, 122–3, 147
Fine Fare, 38–9, 160, 161
First Castle Electronics, 124–5
Fleet Holdings, 4, 68–71
Fleet, Kenneth, 45
'foie gras' tactic, 157
forecasting, 34, 98, 124–5, 134
Forte, Lord, 125
Foster, John, 154–5

GEC, 17, 26, 39–45, 118, 160
Gifford, Michael, 21, 111
Gill, Jack, 129
Gimbels, 25
Glanfield Lawrence, 37

Glynwed, 12
'golden parachutes', 128–9
Golden Wonder, 149
Goldsmith, Sir James, 31, 136
Goodison, Sir Nicholas, 101, 102, 132
Graham, Peter, 138, 139
Granada, 45, 119
Great Northern Investment Trust, 135
Green, Sir Owen, 20–2, 33, 48, 58–9, 107, 111, 161
'greenmail', 31, 116–17, 136
Gregory Securities, 37
Grovewood Securities, 25
Guest Keen & Nettlefold, 108
Guinness, 10, 26, 60–1, 65–6, 69, 82–4, 114–16, 119–21, 149, 154
Guinness Mahon, 134
   Peat, 133–5
Gulliver, James, 26, 59–61, 66, 83, 109, 110, 121, 154

Habitat, 51, 153
Haden, 112–14
Halpern, Ralph, 9, 30, 48–53, 73, 153
Hambro Life, 24, 36–7, 136, 142
Hancock, William, 45
Hanson, Lord, 9–10, 28, 47, 52–8, 76, 93, 109, 152, 156–7
Hanson Brick, 47
   Trust, 9, 26, 47, 54–8, 84, 92, 99, 106, 109, 151–2
Harris, Sir Philip, 29
Harris Queensway, 29, 72
Heron Corporation, 28, 29, 49
Herman's Sporting Goods, 38, 39
Hillsdown Holdings, 11–12
Hiram Walker, 77, 115
Hogg, Christopher, 55
Holden Brown, Sir Derrick, 75, 77
Holloway, J. W., 66
Holmes à Court, Robert, 28, 70, 125, 129
Hongkong & Shanghai Banking Group, 137
Horten, 24
Hutchings, Greg, 78

Imperial Group, 11, 26, 39, 55–8, 84, 99, 106, 109, 120, 121, 129, 149, 151
ICL, 37
Independent Broadcasting Authority, 119
institutions, 1, 21–2, 32, 39, 59, 72, 73, 87, 101–7, 110–11, 126–8, 159
International Stores, 9, 24, 38
investors' protection, 131, 132
IXL, 77

Jacomb, Sir Martin, 143–4
Japan, 7, 51, 133
Jewellers Guild, 24
jobbers, 86, 132–3
junk bonds, 77, 122–3

Kalms, Stanley, 16–17, 71, 73–4, 107
Kent, Geoffrey, 57, 106
Key Markets, 38
Kissin, Lord, 134
Kitcat & Aitken, 135
Kleinwort Benson, 82, 85, 143

Laing & Cruickshank, 141
law/lawyers, 31, 32, 56, 84–5, 87–95, 116, 118–19
Lawson, Nigel, 45
Lazards, 82, 120
Lennons, 38
libel, 42, 57, 118–19, 160
Linklaters & Paine, 91
Littlewoods, 28
Lloyds Bank, 18, 44–5, 93–4, 108, 140–1, 160
London Brick, 47, 54–5, 92, 152
Lonrho Group, 4, 6, 120, 121
Lovell White & King, 89, 92
Lucas, 45
Lyons, J., 74, 110, 115

Mckechnie, 78
McWilliam, Michael, 139, 141
Mace, Dan, 89, 90
MAIBL, 138
management, company, 10, 21, 22, 24, 47, 59, 63–7 passim, 71,

106, 107, 127–9, 145, 161–3
  passim
buyouts, 11, 30, 50, 55, 56,
  112–14
managers, fund, 87, 103–6, 159
Margulies, Ephraim, 11
Marwan, Ashraf, 70
Matthews, Victor, 69, 70
Maxwell, Robert, 3–6, 70–1, 107
Meaney, Sir Patrick, 20–2, 33, 111
Mercantile House, 133, 141–2
Mercury International Group, 96,
  143, 144
Merrill Lynch, 56, 96, 133, 142–3
Midland Bank, 20, 138, 139
Mirror Group, 3, 70, 107
Miquel, Raymond, 121
Monk, Alec, 38–9, 161
Monopolies Commission, 10–12
  passim, 38, 41–5 *passim*, 54,
  57, 60, 66, 77, 91, 94, 118,
  120–1, 123, 137, 145, 147, 149,
  160, 163
Montagu, David, 135
Morgan Crucible, 124–5
Morgan Grampian, 69
Morgan Grenfell, 21, 57, 73, 83–5,
  114–15, 120–1, 160
Morse, Sir Jeremy, 140
Morton, Alistair, 134
Mothercare Group, 51, 153
Mountain, Sir Denis, 23–4
Mulcahy, Geoffrey, 73
Mullens, 96, 143
Murdoch, Rupert, 2–3

National Westminster Bank, 14, 44,
  159
newspapers, 2–6, 69–71
Nomura, 133

Observer, The, 4, 6, 70
Office of Fair Trading, 6, 18, 42, 77,
  91, 119, 120, 145, 147, 151
Oppenheimer, 141

P & O, 117
Packer, Kerry, 136
Parkinson, Cecil, 132, 147
'passing the parcel', 27–32, 70, 114,
  127

Pegler Hattersley, 12, 78
Pepper Lee, 155
Percival, Gordon, 11
Perkins, Dorothy, 50
Pitman, Brian, 141
Plessey, 17, 26, 39–45, 119, 160
'poison pills', 82, 114–16
Powell Duffryn, 55
prices, bid, 8, 14–16, 22, 25–6,
  35–45, 56, 57, 66, 76, 146–8
  passim, share 1, 7, 13–15, 28,
  29, 31–3 *passim*, 36, 43–4, 65,
  68–70, 72–5 *passim*, 77, 104,
  105, 108–9, 125, 127, 128,
  139, 140, 151, 153, 154
Prudential, 22, 103, 106, 110
public relations, 43, 44, 90, 98–100,
  109–10
purchases, share, 57–8, 68, 94, 95,
  97, 101–2, 105, 116, 120, 126,
  150, 160–1

Quayle, David, 72

Racal, 37
Rank Organisation, 21, 30, 110–11,
  114, 119, 127
Reece, Sir Gordon, 43, 44
'refining', 57
regulation, 15–16, 32–3, 74, 82–3,
  85, 88, 94, 95, 97, 98, 115,
  118–20, 122, 129, 147–51, 163
  self-, 119
research, 97
retailing, 8–10, 24, 25, 38–9, 48–52,
  59–60, 71–4, 152–3, 161
Reuters, 70
Richardson, Michael, 55
Rippon, Geoffrey, 134
RIT, 135
Robinson Rentals, 45
Rodgers, Geoffrey, 71
Ronson, Gerald, 28–9, 31, 49, 54,
  70, 72
Rothschild, Evelyn, 135
Rothschild, Jacob, 24–5, 31–2, 37,
  68, 81, 135–7, 142, 162
  Holdings, 81
Rothschild, L. F., Unterberg, Tobin,
  135

Rothschild, N. M., 31, 55, 135
Rowe & Pitman, 39, 96, 97, 143
Rowe, Jeremy, 54
Rowland, Tiny, 3, 4, 6, 70
Royal Bank of Scotland, 18, 136,
    137, 140

Saunders, Ernest, 67, 83, 109, 154
Savoy Hotel Group, 125–6
Scholey, David, 143–4
Schweppes, 44
SCM, 56, 152, 156, 157
Screen Entertainments, 30, 114
Securities and Exchange
    Commission, 42, 56, 93–4
Securities and Investment Board, 81,
    95, 98, 119, 148, 151
Selig, Roger, 109
shareholders, 21, 33, 39, 42, 59,
    94–7, 101–11, 115–16, 121,
    125–8, 150, 161, 162
    pre-emption rights, 39, 126, 150,
    161
    see also institutions
Sheehy, Patrick, 23–5
shell companies, 122–3
Simms Motors, 45
Singer & Friedlander, 82, 134
Slaughter & May, 91
Somerset, 64
South Africa, 138, 152
Spencer, Cyril, 49
Spillers, 99, 120, 121, 129
St Regis, 31, 136
Standard Bank Investment
    Corporation, 138
Standard Chartered, 18, 45, 93, 108,
    137–41, 160
Standard Telephone & Cables, 37
Stevens, David, 71
Stirling, Jeffrey, 117
Stock Conversion, 117
Stock Exchange, 17, 33, 39, 58, 74,
    91–2, 94, 97, 101, 102, 115,
    120, 126, 131–3, 150, 151, 161
    Yellow Book, 94
Stockley, 117
Storehouse Group, 152–3
Strachan, Douglas, 76
Stromberg–Carlson, 42

Takeover Code, 15–16, 32–3, 37, 55,
    68, 81, 83, 85, 88, 90–1, 94,
    95, 99, 115, 123
    Panel, 16, 37, 43, 60, 66, 77,
    79–82, 85–7 passim 95, 99,
    109, 118–20, 122–5 passim,
    129–30, 148, 150, 151, 160
Tate & Lyle, 11–12, 37
Taube, Nils, 135
taxation, 93, 101–2
Tebbitt, Norman, 55
Thorn EMI, 30, 114, 159
Thornton, Robert, 50
Tilling, Thomas, 19–22, 26, 33, 35,
    48, 58–9, 104, 107, 111, 161–2
Today, 3, 5, 6
Tomkins, F. H., 12, 78
Tootal, 31–2, 67–8
Toronto-Dominion Bank of Canada,
    138
Trafalgar House, 4, 69, 113
Trusthouse Forte, 125–6
Tube Investments, 29
Tucson, Arizona, 29
Typhoo Tea, 44

Unilever, 37, 73
Union Bank of California, 93, 139,
    140
unit trusts, 87, 101, 103, 128, 133–5,
    136
United Bankcorp of Arizona, 139
United Biscuits, 26, 39, 57–8, 84, 99,
    106, 120, 121, 149
United Dominion Stores, 9–10, 28,
    50, 54, 93, 152, 156
United Newspapers, 3, 5, 70–1
United States, 2, 7, 20, 25, 27–9, 31,
    42, 56, 84, 85, 93, 101, 116,
    122–3, 126, 128, 139, 142–3,
    160
US Industries, 55

vendor placings, 38–9, 150, 161
Vinelot, Lord Justice, 84
Viyella, 45
voting structure, 125–6

Wagstaff, Alan, 32, 67–8
Walsh, Graham, 83

Warburg, S. G., 19, 21, 82, 83, 85, 96, 133, 143, 144
Wedd Durlacher, 143
Weinberg, Mark, 24–5, 135, 142
Weinstock, Lord, 17, 40–4, 118
Weston, Gary, 38–9
Westpac, 138
White, Sir Gordon, 53, 56
Williams, 78

Williams & Glyns, 137
Wood Mackenzie, 97
Woolworth, 16–17, 28–9, 45, 71–4, 104–5, 160

Xerox Corporation, 110

de Zoete & Bevan, 143